# LIVING IN...
# THE MIDDLE AGES

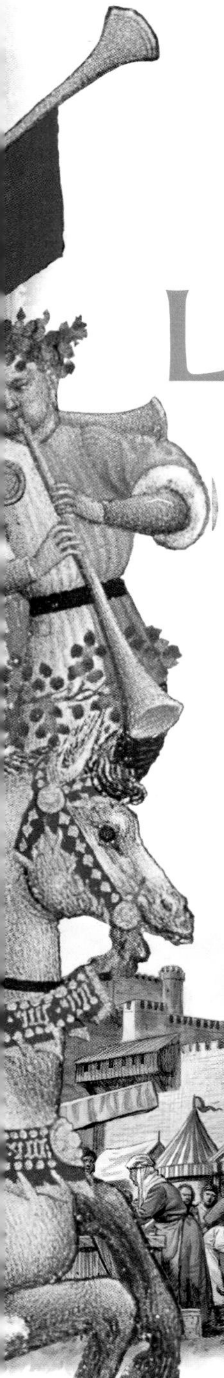

LIVING IN...

# THE MIDDLE AGES

Series consultant editor: Norman Bancroft Hunt

CHELSEA HOUSE PUBLISHERS
An imprint of Infobase Publishing

**LIVING IN THE MIDDLE AGES**



Chelsea House
An imprint of Infobase Publishing
132 West 31st Street
New York, NY 10001

**Library of Congress Cataloging-in-Publication Data**

Bancroft-Hunt, Norman.
Living in the Middle Ages / Norman Bancroft Hunt.
p. cm. — (Living in the ancient world)
Includes index.
ISBN 978-0-8160-6341-3
1. Middle Ages—Juvenile literature. 2. Europe—History—476-1492—Juvenile literature. 3. Europe—Social life and customs—Juvenile literature. 4. Civilization, Medieval—Juvenile literature. I. Title. II. Series.

CB351.B34 2008
909.07—dc22 2008033137

Chelsea House books are available at special discounts when purchased in bulk quantities for businesses, associations, institutions or sales promotions. Please call our Special Sales Department in New York at: (212) 967-8800 or (800) 322-8755.

You can find Chelsea House on the World Wide Web at: http://www.chelseahouse.com

For Thalamus Publishing
Series consultant editor: Norman Bancroft Hunt
Contributors: John Haywood, Angus Konstam, Warren Lapworth
Project editor: Warren Lapworth
Maps and design: Roger Kean

Date printed: April, 2010
Printed and bound in China

10 9 8 7 6 5 4 3 2
This book is printed on acid-free paper

**Picture acknowledgments**
All illustrations by Oliver Frey except for – Roger Kean: 53 (both), 54 (both), 55; Mike White/Temple Rogers: 18–19 (top), 22–23 (below), 24–25, 42–43, 50–51, 60–61, 73, 80–81 (top), 84–85, 86, 88–89, 90–91 (top), 92.

Photographs – Gianni dagli Orti/Corbis: 37 (top), 37 (below), 43 (top), 49, 75; David Reed/Corbis: 54; Archivo Iconografica/Corbis: 40, 43 (below), 47, 52, 60, 87; Arte & Immaginari: 84 (center), 84 (below); Philip de Bay/Corbis: 62–63; Bettman/Corbis: 72 (top); Christies Images/Corbis: 67 (below); Elio Ciol/Corbis: 84 (left); Corbis: 8–9; Franco Frey: 25 (both), 29 (both); Francis G Mayer: 67 (top); Thalamus Publishing: 2, 19, 20, 28, 34, 36, 39, 44–45, 48 (both), 57 (both), 63, 66 (all), 69, 72 (below), 74, 76, 82–83 (all); Nik Wheeler/Corbis: 53.

# CONTENTS

## Place in History

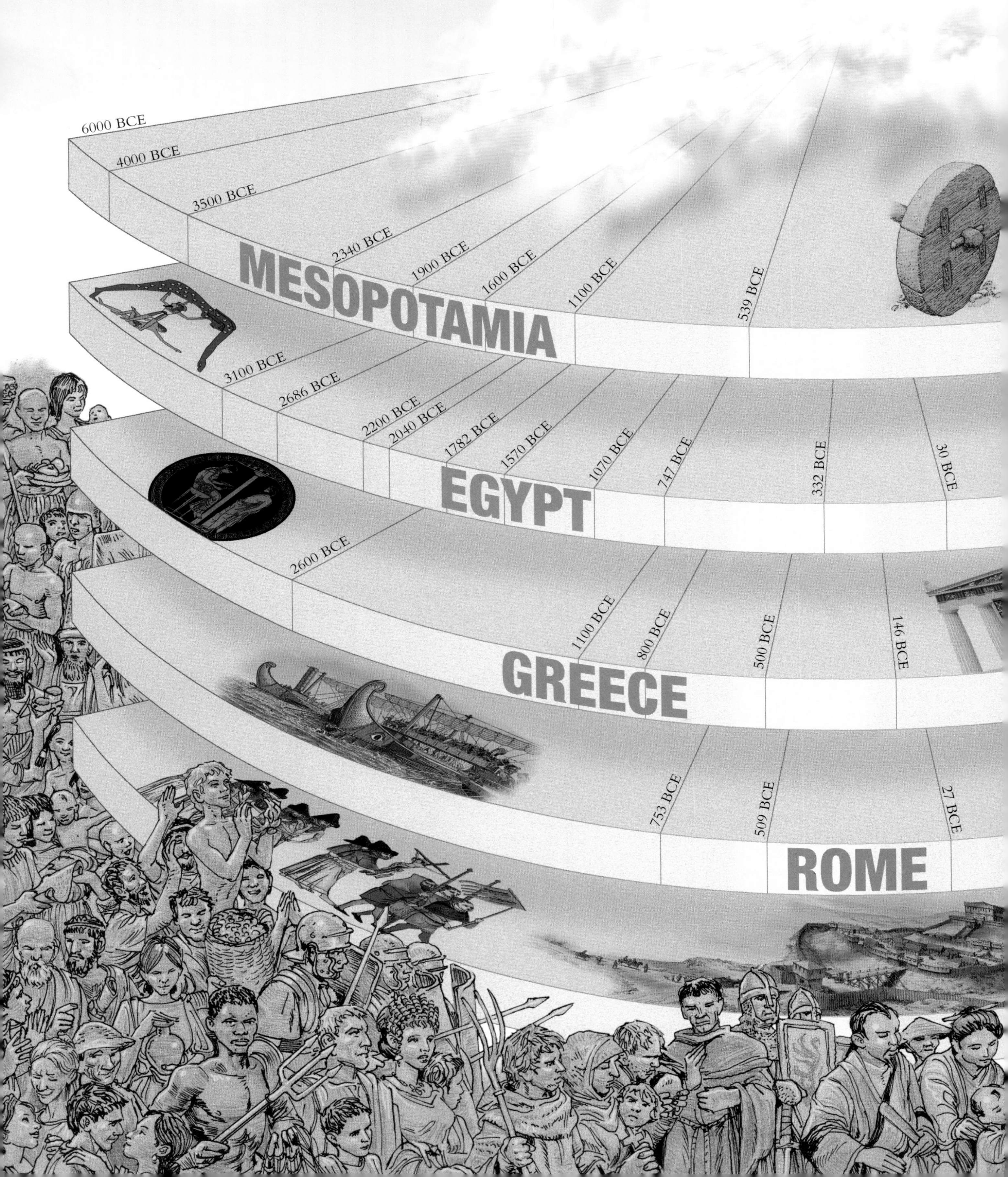
6000 BCE
4000 BCE
3500 BCE
2340 BCE
1900 BCE
1600 BCE
1100 BCE
539 BCE
MESOPOTAMIA
3100 BCE
2686 BCE
2200 BCE
2040 BCE
1782 BCE
1570 BCE
1070 BCE
747 BCE
332 BCE
30 BCE
EGYPT
2600 BCE
1100 BCE
800 BCE
500 BCE
146 BCE
GREECE
753 BCE
509 BCE
27 BCE
ROME

## What the Middle Ages Did for Us

The period called the "Middle Ages" is often portrayed as one of romance, of mighty castles, of chivalrous knights and their elegant ladies, but it was also a time when peasants, through their own efforts, began to assert their rights. While it was still a time of primitive superstition, the Middle Ages gave us the foundations of the modern city and the laws to govern it, the beginnings of modern democracy, a return to a monetary economy, the first banks, the first real books mass-produced on printing presses, and a merchant middle class that would soon promote undreamed of exploration of the world in their perilously small sailing ships.

# Landscape and Climate

From the rainswept Atlantic seaboard to the edges of the Russian hinterland, western Europe is a land of differing regions, divided by mountain ranges and mighty rivers.

1. Dublin
2. London
3. Hamburg
4. Copenhagen
5. Oslo
6. Stockholm
7. Reval (Tallinn)
8. Riga
9. Danzig
10. Lübeck
11. Caen
12. Rouen
13. Paris
14. Cologne
15. Frankfurt
16. Munich
17. Bordeaux
18. Lyon
19. Basel
20. Zurich
21. Arles
22. Genoa
23. Milan
24. Venice
25. La Coruña
26. Oporto
27. Lisbon
28. Cadiz
29. Toledo
30. Málaga
31. Valencia
32. Barcelona
33. Cagliari
34. Florence
35. Ravenna
36. Rome
37. Naples
38. Palermo
39. Syracuse
40. Bari

Europe's climate varies enormously, from north to south and from west to east. The temperature gradient from the Baltic Sea to the Mediterranean is extreme, being warmer further south. To the east, winters are bitterly cold due to the prevailing icy winds from the northern Tundra region, and summers are dry and hot. However, temperatures are kept on a more even keel along the Atlantic seaboard because of the moderating effect of the ocean.

Typically, those countries facing the Atlantic Ocean have a much higher average rainfall than those in the central and eastern areas, which are sheltered by the mountain ranges of the Pyrenees, Alps, and central German highlands. As a result, northwestern Europe is more suited to growing grain and livestock. While England is best suited to raising sheep, France is the great granary.

The mountains have a large effect on both the climate and cultures, naturally dividing one region from another. They are also the watersheds for Europe's great rivers, along which most trade flows in the Middle Ages.

At the start of our story, and with the exception of the more arid regions of the Spanish plateau, approximately 80 percent of Europe is covered by forest. The few roads that exist are little more than mud tracks, and almost everyone is engaged with agriculture in one way or another. Not many people live in the very few small cities—most inhabit widely scattered villages, often of no more than a hundred people. At the start of the medieval period, that's all about to change...

*41.* Ireland
*42.* Scotland
*43.* England and Wales
*44.* France
*45.* German states
*46.* Denmark-Norway
*47.* Sweden
*48.* Baltic states
*49.* Lithuania
*50.* Italian states
*51.* Hungary
*52.* Balkan states
*53.* Balearic Islands
*54.* *North Sea*
*55.* *Baltic Sea*
*56.* *Adriatic Sea*
*57.* *Atlantic Ocean*
*58.* *Mediterranean Sea*
*59.* *Ionian Sea*
*60.* *Tyrrhenian Sea*
*61.* Spanish states

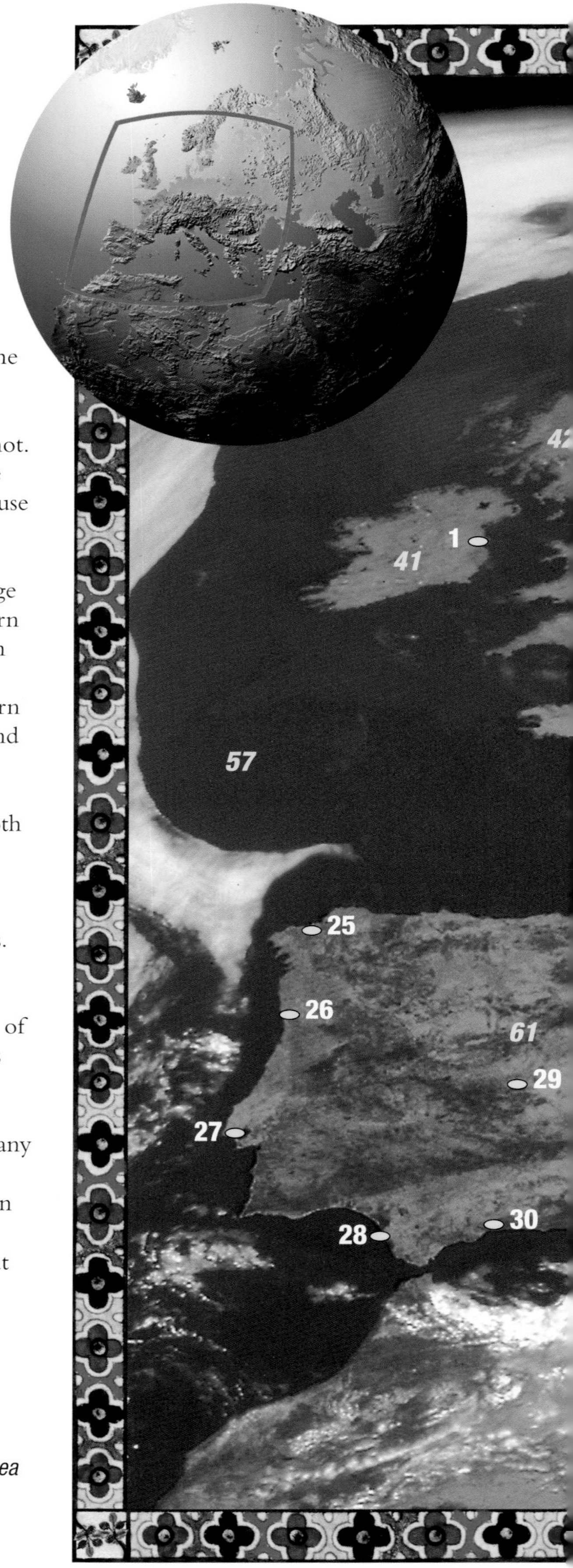

5
6
7
8
46
46
47
48
48
46
54
4
55
3
10
9
48
49
43
2
45
14
12
11
13
15
44
19
20
16
51
17
18
23
24
50
35
21
22
34
36
50
56
52
32
50
37
40
31
50
60
61
52
53
33
58
59
38
61
39
58

# A Brief History of Medieval Europe, 800–1450 CE

While this volume covers the whole period from the late Frankish empire in about 800 CE to the beginnings of the Renaissance in about 1450, it concentrates on two periods in detail—1000 to 1200 and an "ideal" moment in about 1350–1400.

Following the fall of the Roman Empire, Europe faced its bleakest period for centuries as it was occupied by successive waves of invaders. Christianity was almost extinguished, but the faith was kept alive by isolated Celtic and Mediterranean monks who ensured its survival.

A series of Gothic, Saxon, and Frankish states emerged in western Europe. The eventual dominance of the Franks in northwestern Europe created a degree of stability. The conversion of the Franks to Christianity took place just as Muslims were invading Spain, and much of the Iberian peninsula remained in the hands of these "Moors" for most of the Middle Ages.

## Unity of the Holy Roman Empire

The Merovingian and Carolingian dynasties of the Frankish kingdom halted the Muslim advance, and under Charlemagne (r.768–814) the Franks created an empire that unified western Europe culturally and politically. Although this unity was short-lived, it was encouraged by the Roman Catholic Church.

In 800 the institution of the Holy Roman Empire was created when Pope Leo III crowned Charlemagne "Roman Emperor." This politically minded move split western Europe from the Byzantine east, whose emperor claimed sovereignty over all of Europe as the direct successor of the ancient Roman rulers.

For centuries to come, Holy Roman Emperors and later French kings would battle with each other for dominance of Italy—sometimes allied to the pope, sometimes against him. At the start of the period, much of Italy was dominated by the Lombards, another Germanic "barbarian" race. Soon enough, the southern regions came under the thumb of Norman invaders and became a battleground between Normans, Byzantines, and Germans.

## The Normans and feudalism

The Normans were descendants of Vikings who settled the region of France around the mouth of the River Seine in about 900. They created the Duchy of Normandy, in theory subject to

The Crusades were a defining event of the Middle Ages. For 200 years between 1096 and 1291, Europe poured nobles, knights, and armed retinues by the thousands to recover Jerusalem and the Holy Land from Muslims. In the end, it was a failure and among some unhappy examples, the saddest was that of the Children's Crusade of 1212. Most never made it beyond the heel of Italy, prey to slavers and starvation.

the Frankish kingdom, but in reality quite independent.

Norman adventurers began invading Italy in about 1050, and famously Duke William of Normandy conquered Anglo-Saxon England in 1066. The Normans and their Angevin successors were great castle-builders, inspiring a spate of building in all parts of Europe that saw stone towers appear on almost every suitable hilltop.

It was the Normans who developed feudalism to its peak (*see page 14*). This system of obligation lasted until almost the end of the Middle Ages, finally overthrown by the demands of a growing middle class of merchants and skilled craftsmen.

The feudal system took root throughout western Europe, although the way it operated altered from region to region. While France and England were similar, the numerous rulers of the patchwork German states kept the peasantry in something approaching slavery. The local rulers also kept themselves more aloof of their overlord, the Holy Roman Emperor. His was an elected position, unique in medieval Europe.

## Fighting France

France's story during the Middle Ages was one of the king struggling to dominate his virtually independent barons. Unity was needed to drive the English from their vast holdings in the old Frankish kingdom.

These were the hereditary Norman lands and those of the Angevin (or Plantagenet) dynasty that followed through intermarriage, which originated from the region of southwestern France.

The pope or an archbishop anoints a king with oil at his coronation. The oil symbolizes that the monarch has received God's grace from his representative on Earth. It also gives popes a claim to rule the king, a source of much conflict throughout the Middle Ages.

Eventually, the French kings gained ascendancy over their nobles, and the Hundred Year's War (1337–1453) ended English dominion on the Continent.

## A growing spate of urbanization

Although there were differences in the peoples, languages, and cultures across Europe, there were many similarities. The Roman Catholic Church was the great defining power and, in theory at least, from peasant to king, everyone owed allegiance to the pope in Rome as spiritual head of the Church and God's representative on Earth.

In 800, much of Europe was forested, its low population widely scattered, mostly peasants tied to the lands of their overlords. By the end of the Middle Ages Europe had changed beyond recognition. Most of the forests were gone, cleared for grazing land and to provide timber for building towns and the growing merchant fleets and navies.

Towns came to dominate the economy and culture. No matter the means of wealth, from Germany to Italy, from England to France and Spain (beginning to emerge from Muslim dominance), the new towns prospered through the efforts of a growing middle class of merchants, fueled by cheap labor, and financed by the new banks of Germany and northern Italy.

All over the Continent, universities had appeared, sponsoring a passion for learning and acting as a unifying force between many different countries. With the new knowledge came discoveries of ancient Greek and Roman teaching, and the way was paved for the cultural Renaissance.

# Table of Major Dates

| All dates CE | 800 | 900 | 1000 | 1050 | 1100 |
|---|---|---|---|---|---|
| **PEOPLE AND CULTURE** | • Jewish merchants in Lombardy open the first bank/money repository, 808<br>• Vikings discover Iceland, 861<br>• Technique of nailed-on horseshoes invented, 890 | • Abbey of Cluny established in France, 910<br>• St. Bernard's Hospice founded in Switzerland, 962<br>• Olaf Skutkonung is first Swedish king to accept Christianity, 993 | • Dawn of the new millennium creates widespread terror; people think it is the Day of Judgment<br>• Lief Eriksson discovers the North American continent, 1000<br>• Musical scales introduced by Guido d'Arezzo, 1027 | • Welsh epic poem the *Mabinogion* is written, 1050<br>• Work begins on Westminster Abbey in London, 1052<br>• Appearance of Halley's Comet recorded in Bayeux Tapestry, 1066<br>• Start of the Investiture Crisis that damages authority of the Holy Roman Empire, 1075 (until 1172)<br>• Construction begun on the Tower of London, 1078<br>• *The Domesday Book* compiled, first survey of the Middle Ages, 1087<br>• First Cistercian monastery founded in Citeaux, France, 1098 | • The First Miracle (Passion) Play is performed, 1110<br>• St. Bernard founds a monastery at Clairvaux, 1115<br>• First trade guilds are recorded, 1120<br>• Pope recognizes the religious military Order of the Knights Templar, 1128<br>• Work begins on revolutionary Gothic abbey church of St. Denis in Paris, 1132<br>• Chartres Cathedral built on Gothic lines, 1145<br>• First mention of Russia in historic documents, 1147 |
| **MILITARY AND POLITICS** | • Charlemagne crowned Roman Emperor, 800<br>• Vikings raid French coast as far south as the Loire estuary, 814<br>• Kenneth MacAlpine founds a unified Scotland, 844<br>• Danes attack the Anglo-Saxon kingdom of Wessex, 871<br>• Alfred defeats the Danes, 878, England divided between the Danelaw to the north and Wessex in the south<br>• Viking fleet besieges Paris, but is driven off by Charles the Fat, 887 | • Magyars enter Germany, 907<br>• Franks recognize a small area of the Seine estuary as the Duchy of Normandy under Viking Hrolf (Rollo) the Ganger, 911<br>• Rollo annexes all of Normandy, 923<br>• Battle of Lechfeld ends Magyar threat to western Europe, 955<br>• First record of silver mining in Germany's Harz mountains, 964 | • First persecution of heretics by the Church, 1012<br>• Danes conquer England, 1014<br>• Norman adventurers act as mercenaries in Italy, 1015<br>• Navarre annexes Castile in Spain, 1028<br>• Macbeth of Moray kills Duncan in battle at Elgin, Scotland, 1040 | • Norman kingdom established in southern Italy, 1053<br>• Macbeth, King of Scots, is killed by his rival Malcolm, 1057<br>• Duke William of Normandy defeats King Harold at Hastings and conquers England, 1066<br>• Normans begin conquest of Sicily, 1072<br>• Toledo in Spain recaptured from the Muslims, 1081<br>• First Crusade begins, 1096<br>• Crusaders capture Jerusalem, 1099 | • Stephen of Boulogne seizes the English crown on the death of his uncle, Henry I. Civil war breaks out, 1135<br>• Start of Hohenstaufen dynasty in Germany, 1138<br>• Second Crusade ends in failure, 1149 |

*The peak of Crusader castles, Krak des Chevaliers.*

| 1200 | 1250 | 1300 | 1350 | 1400 | 1450 |
|---|---|---|---|---|---|
| Council of Cathar eretics formed in outhern France, 167<br>Foundation of xford University, ngland, 1167<br>Romantic verse *ancelot* is written, 168<br>Thomas à Becket urdered in Canterbury athedral, 1170<br>First recorded indmill in western urope, 1180<br>*Reynard the Fox* is ritten, 1186, a French ble that influenced ter writers<br>First Florin minted in orence, 1189<br>Teutonic Order of nights founded, 1190 | • Foundation of Cambridge University, 1200<br>• Wolfram von Eschenback writes of knights and chivalry in *Parzifal*, 1203<br>• Francis of Assisi founds the Franciscan Order of monks, 1209<br>• Gottfried von Strassburg writes *Tristan und Isolde*, 1210<br>• Danes adopt the first national flag in Europe, 1218<br>• Foundation of Naples University in Italy, 1224<br>• Roger Bacon first records gunpowder in Europe, 1249 | • Minting of gold coins begins, 1252<br>• Birth of the painter Giotto in Florence, Italy, first of the new "Renaissance" artists, 1267<br>• The Venetian Marco Polo starts his 24-year journey to China, 1271<br>• English philosopher Roger Bacon is imprisoned for heresy, 1277<br>• The romantic poem *Lohengrin* is written, 1285<br>• Spectacles are invented, 1290<br>• First mechanical clocks recorded, 1270 | • Dante's *Divine Comedy* is written, c.1300<br>• Birth of Italian poet and humanist thinker Francesco Petrarca (Petrarch), 1304<br>• Giotto paints his frescos in Padua, Italy, 1305<br>• Birth of Italian humanist writer Giovanni Boccaccio, 1313<br>• Construction is begun on the Papal Palace at Avignon in France, 1334<br>• Hanseatic League dominates Baltic trade, 1344<br>• Approximately 24 million die in the Black Death, 1346–50 | • Black Death ends after ravaging most of Europe, 1350<br>• First marine insurance begins in Genoa, c.1350<br>• Hans Fugger founds a bank in Augsburg, Germany, 1380<br>• Theologian Wycliffe is expelled from Oxford and his first translation into English of the Bible condemned, 1382<br>• Geoffrey Chaucer writes the *Canterbury Tales*, 1346–1400<br>• King addresses parliament in English rather than French for first time, 1367<br>• Construction on the Bastille fortress in Paris begins, 1369 | • Italian architect Filippo Brunelleschi produces his *Rules of Perspective*, 1412<br>• The Medici of Florence become papal bankers, 1414<br>• Joan of Arc relieves the siege of Orléans, 1429<br>• Portuguese sailors explore Africa's west coast, 1434<br>• Birth of Leonardo da Vinci, 1452<br> |
| Frederick I arbarossa 152–90) becomes oly Roman Emperor<br>Frederick arbarossa sacks ilan in Italy, 1162<br>Henry II of England ormally annexes eland, 1171<br>Saladin recaptures erusalem for the uslims, 1187<br>Third Crusade is roclaimed, 1189<br><br>*lonks kept alive the hristian faith and the kills of reading and riting.* | • Fourth Crusade turns from the Holy Land to sack Constantinople, 1204<br>• King John of England agrees to make England a papal fief, 1213<br>• King John signs the *Magna Carta*, creating rudiments of a parliamentary system, 1215<br>• Pope orders the creation of the Inquisition to end heresy, 1233 | • Byzantines recapture Constantinople from the fading Latin empire, 1261<br>• Muslim armies capture Acre, the last Christian stronghold in Palestine, marking the end of successful crusades, 1291<br>• Edward I's "Model Parliament" summons knights and burghers from English shires and towns to participate in government decisions, 1295 | • The papacy is moved from Rome to Avignon, 1305<br>• The English capture and execute Scottish rebel William Wallace, 1305<br>• Robert the Bruce defeats Edward II at Bannockburn and makes Scotland independent, 1314<br>• Swiss defeat Habsburg dynasty at Morgarten, 1315<br>• Start of the Hundred Years War between England and France, 1337<br>• Persecution of Jews gathers pace in Germany, 1348 | • English victory over the French at Poiters temporarily halts the Hundred Year's War, 1356<br>• Hundred Year's War is renewed, 1369<br>• Start of the "Great Schism" when two and then three opposing popes existed, 1378–1414<br>• The Peasants' Revolt is led by Watt Tyler in England, 1381 | • Owen Glyndwr proclaims himself Prince of Wales and rebels against England, 1400<br>• French are decisively defeated by the English at Agincourt, 1415<br>• The English burn Joan of Arc at the stake in Rouen, 1431<br>• The English are defeated by the French at Castillon, ending the Hundred Years War, 1453<br>• Start of the Wars of the Roses between the Lancaster and York dynasties of England, 1455 |

CHAPTER 1

# Working for the Overlord

## A Life of Obligations

Beset by enemies—Magyars from the east, Moors from the south, and Vikings from the north—the Franks have developed a social and military system that offers protection against external threat. This structure is known as the feudal system.

The word feudal comes from the Latin *feudum,* or fief (estate). A fief is a parcel of land held by an individual in return for his allegiance and military commitment to his feudal superior. The roots of feudalism go back to the barbarian invasions during the last years of the Roman Empire.

The holding of a piece of land in return for certain obligations was common under Roman law, while the fealty (an oath of loyalty) sworn by an inferior to his superior is a Germanic tribal tradition. Feudalism simply combines the two practices.

The feudal system is a pyramid, with the king or a duke at the top and the mass of peasants at its base. From top to bottom, feudalism is based around military service. Beneath the king or duke come the powerful nobles—barons and then counts—and lower down the scale the many lesser knights.

### Protection at a price

The minor lords and knights are mounted warriors, who need to own the resources to supply horses, armor, and equipment. They are required to devote most of their time to military service.

In return, their overlord grants them land as a fief, including all the peasants living there. The peasants, called serfs or *villeins*, are virtual slaves of their lord, and toil in the fields to create the wealth the knight needs to fulfill his feudal obligations.

In times of war, the knight conscripts many of his serfs to take up arms as infantrymen to fight for the king or duke. This forced conscription is part of their obligation to their lord. In return, the lord must offer his serfs protection, so that they can sow and harvest the fields in safety and raise children.

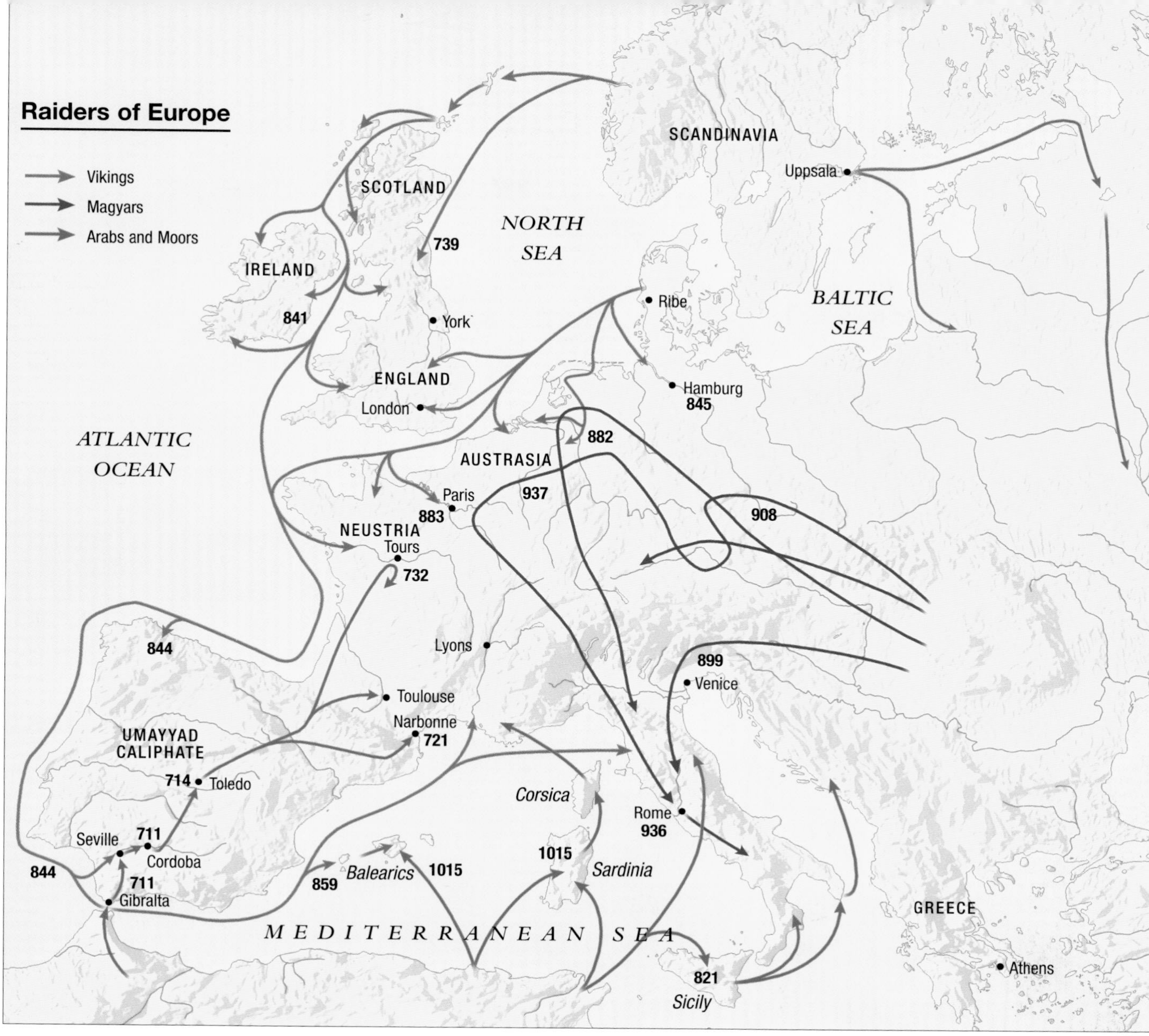


## Servants of a higher authority

In the war-torn Middle Ages, free farmers lack the means to defend their own lands, and so many seek the protection of a knight. Unfortunately, this means exchanging their freeholding status for serfdom, but at least it ensures survival.

In theory, it is the king or duke who grants a knight his fief, but in practice many lesser knights lack the resources to defend their land against large invasions. In this case, they often surrender their lands to a more powerful count or baron. In turn, this overlord grants the fief back to the knight, who becomes his vassal, or subject ("vassal" comes from the Latin *vassus*, meaning servant).

In theory, the king is the feudal overlord, but in reality his barons are supreme in their own fiefs. Many kings are little more than figureheads. Barons administer their own estates, dispense their own justice, levy taxes and tolls, and demand military service from their vassals. Often, the barons can field greater armies than the king.

## The Catholic Church apart

In the Middle Ages, the Church stands apart from the feudal system by not being a vassal of king or noble. Under the Carolingian kings—who adopted some aspects of Roman government—Church lands were given special privileges, which have been maintained.

Bishops may operate separately from royal authority. They can also pass local laws, own the serfs working on their land, and raise tithes (taxes) as they see fit.

**Far left:** The feudal pyramid of power—from mighty king or duke down the ranks to the lowly serfs.

# The Early Medieval Village

**At the heart of every fief is the village—a community where the *villeins* live. It is usually situated close by the local knight's castle, to offer service and receive his protection.**

Ludford is a fictitious but authentic early medieval village. There are various reasons for its siting, but the most important is that the castle guards a ford, which crosses the river at the highest point barges can reach from the nearby sea. The road here is an old Roman route, and much trade is carried along it. The knight can increase his wealth by charging a toll on all merchants traveling north or south on the road.

Ludford's lord is Sir Edmund, a knight of some eminence, and his manor (*see "Lord of the manor"*) boasts a castle of a type called motte and bailey (*see pages 26–27*), a simple affair built on the low rising hill beyond the village. The land around the river crossing was cleared long ago during Roman times and provides plenty of fertile ground for farming.

## Everyone is a farmer

Ludford's population is less than a hundred men, women, and children. Almost all of them work in the fields, although some women and a few men are also employed in the castle, doing menial jobs in the stables and kitchen.

Some of the population are peasant farmers, who rent their land from either the local priest or from Sir Edmund, the rest are his serfs.

Children are also expected to toil in the fields, with the youngest looking after the pigs and poultry. There is no school, since no one needs to be able to read, write, or count any more than a handful of farm animals.

**1.** Ancient Roman road, now fallen into disrepair.

**2.** Ford across the river, with the lord's tollgate.

**3.** Huts of the villagers.

**4.** Chapel and priest's hut, and behind it the "tithe barn."

**5.** The lord-knight's motte-and-bailey castle.

**6.** Benedictine monastery.

## Religious observance

Ludford has a small church and a priest who lives in a hut beside it. He also acts as chaplain to the castle, and survives on the rent from peasants living on the nearby church lands, tithes from the villagers, as well as a small stipend (salary) from the knight.

However, the monastery at some distance from the village also provides religious counsel. Its monks share the knight's revenue from tolls and exact tithes (*see pages 48–49*) on the villagers in return for providing medical care.

Beyond the outskirts of the village, the dark forest closes in, isolating Ludford from its nearest neighbors miles away.

## The peasant's hut

At this stage of its development, Ludford consists of about 30 families living in rough huts. These are typically of one or two rooms (*see page 20*), constructed of simple timber frames filled in with dried turf or "wattle and daub"—a screen of small branches covered in a mud made from soil and cow dung, whitewashed after drying out. The floor is just stamped-down dirt. A portion of the house is divided off as a "byre" to stable the livestock in winter.

The roof is a thatch of straw or river rushes. There are neither chimneys nor real windows. Smoke from the hearth escapes through a hole in the roof. Furnishings are few—simple stools, a trestle table, and beds on the floor made from rushes, straw, or leaves.

### Lord of the manor

From the Latin *manere* (to remain, or dwell), manor is the term that describes a feudal lord's estate. A manor consists of a fortified manor house (or castle), one or more villages, and up to several thousand acres of land divided into meadow, pasture, cultivated fields, and forest.

The farm land is divided into three—about half for the lord of the manor, about a third for the church, and the remainder for the peasants and serfs. Peasants who rent land, called a croft, pay for it by giving at least half of every week to work for the lord and the church.

# A Peasant's Life in the Farming Year

The turning seasons mark the basic rhythm of people's lives. The time of year determines what they do, the length of the working day, and what they eat.

This is an agricultural world in which as much as 90 percent of the population is engaged in farming. The weather shapes the lives of the serfs, and determines the outcome of the harvest—and whether people will survive or die of famine. While the Church marks the New Year on January 1, for the medieval peasant Lady Day, March 25, is the start of their New Year. It is the time when work in the field begins in earnest after the winter lull.

The winter months are far from idle, however. December is occupied with mending tools, carrying out maintenance, and caring for the confined animals. Dung from the barns is stockpiled and mixed with marl (a clay rich in lime used as fertilizer) and spread on the fields. Unfortunately, there is never enough to fertilize more than the closest strips.

## The spring planting

The fields are made up of long strips, and divided into fertile and fallow fields. In order to give the soil time to recover its fertility, fields are left fallow, or unplanted, for a year, which means only half of the available ground can be used for crops. However, the concept of crop rotation is catching on and improving yields (*see "The three-field system"*).

The first plowing starts in April when the soil is soft enough to turn easily. A wheeled plow is used on sandy soil, but in heavy clay areas the "moulboard" plow is preferred. The moulboard, mounted on the right-hand side behind the plowshare, turns over the cut earth. The heavy plow is pulled by up to eight oxen or heavy horses, guided by a plowman. Each team is expected to plow an acre a day.

Behind the plowmen come the sowers planting barley, oats, peas, and beans. The seed is protected by covering it with soil by "harrowing." A harrow is effectively a large wooden rake which is dragged over the planted ground.

A harrow is used for breaking up the soil and covering over seeds. It has between four and six wooden beams called bulls, into which are set wooden pegs projecting down to rake the earth. The bulls are joined together by wooden crossbeams.

A moulboard plow produces a deep furrow and turns earth that the coulter blade and plowshare have cut through the surface.

### The three-field system

One simple agricultural improvement has been the change from a two- to a three-field system, where one field is planted with winter grain, one with spring grain, and the third is left fallow, ready for use in the following year. This crop rotation system improves a village's production during the year by about one third.

Improved horse harnesses and the introduction of horseshoes has also increased the efficiency of plowing teams over those using oxen, and horses are becoming more widely used in farming.

**Above:** This illustration from a manuscript of about 1050 shows serfs using a hoe and long-handled scythes to cut grain in August.

Following the plowman, the sower scatters seed from a box. He is followed by a harrow and boys with slings to stone the hungry rooks and crows.

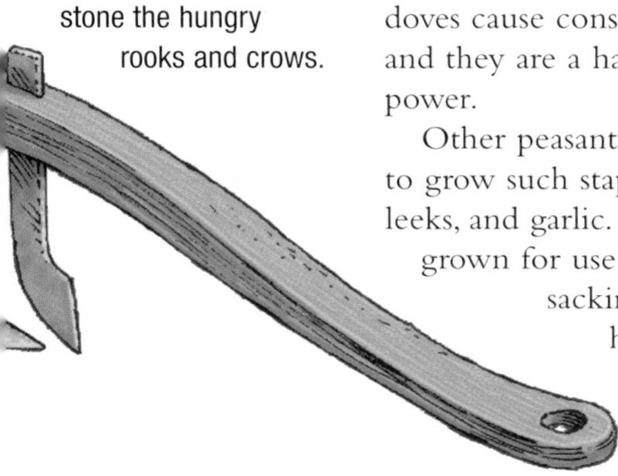

Planting continues into May, and children with slings defend the newly-sown seed from birds. Only the lord's doves are safe, since killing one brings a heavy penalty. The doves cause considerable damage to crops and they are a hated symbol of the lord's power.

Other peasants attend to the gardens, used to grow such staples as cabbages, onions, leeks, and garlic. Flax and hemp are also grown for use in making cloth, rope, and sacking. Culinary and medicinal herbs include parsley, fennel, celery, camomile, mint, summer savory, catmint, mustard, opium poppy, and coriander (cilantro).

## Summer activities

Haymaking is the main activity of June, and involves almost everyone in the village. Teams of haymakers, using long-handled scythes, cut the grass close to the ground. Women and children follow behind them turning the hay to ensure it dries evenly. Finally, the hay is gathered into large stacks.

The hay crop is vital to the village. It provides the main winter fodder for animals and a good crop means a steady supply of fresh meat over winter, a good supply of breeding stock, or a surplus for sale.

As the summer progresses, the main task is weeding with hoes or a pair of long-handled sticks, one with a Y-fork at the end and the other with a small sickle blade. Used together, they cut the stem of the weed at ground level.

The peasants go hungry in July. Grain stores and vegetables are at their lowest and many peasants eke out their diet by foraging in the forest, some of the more daring by poaching their lord's game.

## Harvest time

Weather permitting, the main grain harvest begins in August. Several weeks of warm sun and gentle rain are required for a good crop to grow, but also several dry sunny days are needed to bring the harvest in.

Wheat is harvested with a sickle and cut just below the ear of corn, leaving the long stubble standing in the field. A team of five—four reapers and a binder—can harvest two acres of crops in a day. In a process known as "gleaning," some peasants are granted the right to pick up any grain that falls to the ground during harvesting. This is done before livestock is released to graze the stubble. Gleaning rights are hotly contested because they are of considerable benefit to the recipients.

Apple picking in a French medieval village. The lord, with his bailiff, checks on the progress the serfs are making in picking his apples.

## Into the fall

In September, other crops such as peas and beans are picked, and the grain is processed. It is first threshed with a flail to separate the individual grains from the ears and then winnowed to remove the chaff and straw. This is done by throwing the grains on a winnowing sheet and letting the wind blow the lighter chaff and straw away. The chaff and straw is collected to use as animal fodder.

Church tithes—one sheaf in every ten—are collected from the field before the peasants take the crop to the lord's barns (*see page 23*). Carefully stored and kept free from vermin—a difficult task—the grain will last for several years. Because flour is much harder to keep, the grain is only milled when required for making bread.

Toward the end of September and throughout October, swineherds drive their pigs into the woods to forage for acorns, a means of fattening them up for slaughter. Martinmas (November 11) is the traditional day for slaughtering and salting pigs and older livestock to provide a supply of meat for the coming winter.

Little of the animals is wasted. The flesh provides meat, most of which is preserved by salting or smoking it. The skin is cured (preserved) into tough leather, the bones dried for making needles and pins, or boiled to make glue. Even the blood is carefully saved to make blood puddings.

In mid-November it is time to collect firewood from the forest. The serfs are forbidden from taking anything but dead wood for their own use, and the amount they are allowed to take is limited. Peat is also cut from the wettest sections of the river meadows and stacked to dry for the winter fire. Other serfs cut reeds to be dried for roof thatching.

The success of the harvest will determine how the people fare during the harsh winter months before it is time to prepare the fields for the next year's sowing.

**1.** Thatch roof of straw or river reeds, with an open end to allow smoke to escape.

**2.** Wattle and daub wall.

**3.** Simple furnishings: three-legged stools, trestle table, and a straw bed on the floor.

**4.** Wall dividing off the animals' byre.

A cheese mold and butter churn. Butter is made freshly from cow's milk, but cheese curds are allowed to mature in the mold.

## The medieval peasant's diet

Serf or peasant, the diet is unchanging. The staples are coarse unleavened black bread, peas porridge, and a broth of stewed root vegetables called pottage. Pottage is a soup-stew made from oats, occasionally flavored with beans, peas, turnips, parsnips, or leeks.

There is very little meat in the diet, and most protein is obtained from butter and cheese made from cows' milk. Since the choicest cuts of any freshly slaughtered animal go to the lord of the manor, the peasants are left with the bones and gristle. Of this, they hash and mash the fatty pork, stringy mutton, or tough chicken (only after passing egg-laying stage) into soggy stews. Their teeth are worn to stumps from gnawing bones and munching coarse grains, which usually contain grit from the flour grinding.

## Adding to the diet

Although there is little free time in the working week, a few men manage to slip down to the river bank in early evenings in the hope of a catch. Fish is fried or stewed, as well as smoked or salted to preserve it for the winter.

Pigs are sent out to forage.

The peasant crofter can grow such seasonal vegetables in his garden as lettuces, beans, radishes, carrots, turnips, and onions. Most keep a few scrawny chickens that provide tiny eggs, but the serf is reduced to taking eggs from the nests of any and all wild birds—from swans to sparrows. Fruit trees and bushes provide apples, pears, plums, and berries, but most of this supply belongs to the lord or the priest, so only a small amount of fruit finds its way into the peasant's diet.

The common drink is ale, an alcoholic concoction made from grain, water, and fermented with yeast. In some regions, a more expensive beer is also available, the difference between medieval ale and beer being that beer also uses hops as a flavoring.

## Peasants' clothing

The clothing of peasants and serfs is generally made from rough wool or linen made from flax fibers. Women spin wool into threads and weave a coarse cloth. It is rare for any peasant to own more than two sets of clothing.

Men wear a tunic, with long stockings or leggings, while women wear long gowns with sleeveless tunics and a simple form of wimple to cover the head. Sheepskin cloaks and woolen hats and mittens are worn in winter to protect against the cold. For those who can afford them, linen undergarments protect the skin from the scratchy outer clothing.

The base coloring of cloth is a russet (brown), so most clothing is a drab combination of browns, reds, and grays, with only small variations. Both men and women wear wooden clogs or shoes made of thick cloth or leather. Leather boots are soled and covered with wooden patens (plates) to keep the feet dry. Children's clothing is simply a miniature version of their parents'.

Outer clothes are almost never laundered, but linen underwear does get a regular washing. The tunics and leggings smell of sweat and the wood smoke that permeates fabric in the poorly ventilated huts.

The women grow seasonal vegetables in the small croft garden.

# Local Medieval Government

**The oppressed peasants and virtually enslaved serfs are further burdened by the obligations they owe to their lord and the Church. Both powers rely on the "reeve" to make sure people work hard, obey the rules, and pay their taxes.**

Before the Norman conquest of England in 1066, Germanic Anglo-Saxons lived in rural communities called *tuns* (from which the word "town" is derived). A *tun* comprised a group of ten families called *tithings*, or "tens." In turn, *tithings* were grouped in blocks of ten, called *hundreds*, and collectively the *hundreds* formed into geographically based divisions known by the Anglo-Saxon word *scir*, which means, "a piece cut off."

The Normans altered the pronunciation, *scir* became "shire," and they loosely adopted the boundaries of the shires as feudal fiefs. They did much the same in France and Italy.

Raising the "hue and cry," the reeve is joined by a posse of villagers.

## The reeve's responsibilities

The Anglo-Saxons appointed a *gerefa* (guardian) for each hundred, which the Normans now call a "reeve." Each lord of the manor has his own reeve, who supervises the work of the serfs and guards against any laziness or cheating. The baronial overlord's reeve is an important person because he looks after the whole shire. His title is "shire reeve," or sheriff.

Like others of his station, the reeve of Ludford has a police responsibility to the lord of the manor. He has authority to raise the "hue and cry" for the pursuit of thieves and other criminals. The hue and cry is a communal posse in which all who hear the cry that a crime has been committed are bound by honor to join the pursuit until the villain is captured.

The reeve is also responsible for overseeing the collection of his lord's taxes and tolls, as well as enforcing the Church tithes. In return, he is allowed to keep a portion of each and also enjoys the benefit of choice farming acreage and the use of serfs to work it.

The church's great tithe barn is one of the largest structures in Ludford. Winnowed grain is taken to one of the mills for grinding at no cost to the priest.

A spell in the village stocks for wrongdoers is an unpleasant experience.

## The role of the Church

The Church dominates everybody's life because it is the representative of God's earthly power (*see page 46*). At every level of medieval society, people are gripped by their utter belief in the physical reality of Heaven and Hell. Since it is common knowledge that the only way to reach the heavenly paradise after death is with the blessing of the Roman Catholic Church, everyone does their best to honor their obligations to the Church.

As a result, the Church has total control over the people. One such obligation is to work unpaid on Church lands. For the serfs who also have to devote a portion of their time to working in their lord's fields, this is an extra hardship, using time that could be better spent working on their own plots, producing food for their families.

## A religious tax

In addition, both serfs and free peasants pay to their local church about 10 percent of what they produce in a year—a form of tax called a tithe. Because there is almost no coinage in circulation, tithes are paid in seeds, harvested grain, fruit, or livestock.

The produce that forms the tithe is kept in huge tithe barns. Failure to pay may result in arrest by the reeve and subsequent punishment—the stocks and floggings are common. In addition, the priest tells the offender that his soul will certainly go to Hell unless he does religious penance (*see pages 46–47*).

## Hatched, matched, and dispatched

The Church is involved at every stage of a person's life. Even the poorest must pay a priest for the baptism of their children, which is essential because the unbaptized are unable to pass the portals of Heaven.

To remain unmarried is considered sinful, and again the priest must be paid to bless the ceremony. In order to reach Heaven, burial in holy ground is essential, and church burials are a heavy cost for families.

However you look at it, the Roman Catholic Church receives wealth from every quarter—so much in fact, that its disposable income far outreaches that of the king. And as well as that, it is exempt from taxes.

A priest joins the hands of a couple during a wedding. Early medieval marriages are secular affairs—a priest is not needed to officiate, but by the 14th century the Church makes it unlawful to wed out of church.

# The Manor House

**While the most powerful lords live in large castles—either older ones or newly constructed ones, built with the king's permission—the lesser nobility prefers the extra comfort afforded by a manor house.**

Manor houses vary in size, reflecting the lord's wealth and status. They often comprise several buildings and are mainly self-sufficient, with serfs growing the lord's food and keeping his livestock in the grounds surrounding the house. Because the times are uncertain, the manor house is often fortified, and while the defenses will not keep out an army, they are sufficient to give the lord, his family, and servants protection against bandits and smaller raiding groups.

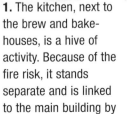

**1.** The kitchen, next to the brew and bake-houses, is a hive of activity. Because of the fire risk, it stands separate and is linked to the main building by a passage way.

**2.** The dovecote.

**3.** The buttery and pantry, with a guest chamber above.

**4.** The chaplain has his own room above the entrance to the hall.

**5.** Guests gather in the great hall, ready for the feast.

**6.** The lord and lady's private chamber, reached via a staircase from the hall.

**7.** The private chapel.

**8.** Storerooms at ground level, where the lord keeps his luxury goods and valuables.

**9.** Outbuildings line the walled courtyard. They provide room for stores, arms, servants, and dogs.

**10.** The fortified manor's gatehouse.

**Top:** Stokesay's north end, with the lord's private apartments on top, surrounding wall, and the later timber-framed gatehouse (built in the 17th century). The great hall, seen here **(center)** from the east, links the private apartments to the tower keep, with its separate entrance.

## Stokesay Castle

Despite its name, Stokesay in England is a fortified manor house—a fine example of the more luxurious living available to the lord of a manor than a drafty castle can offer. Its owner—a leading wool merchant—is a wealthy man. He built Stokesay to impress his business partners as much with the elegance of his house as with its strength.

At the southern end there is a three-story tower topped by battlements—a place of security for the family to retire in case of

hostilities. The lord's private apartments are situated at the northern end, and include a large solar (*see page 33*) with unusually large windows. These are set up high to make it difficult for an attacker to reach, and are protected by arrow slits beneath. The windows let in plenty of light while not harming the house's defensive capabilities.

In between is a great hall for entertaining, with heavy wooden shutters to secure them in case of attack. Stokesay also has a defensive outer wall running in a semi-circle from the north end to the tower, with a gatehouse in its center. Beyond the wall, a wet moat is supplied from a pond.

**Development of the manor house**
These plans show the same building at different periods. The house starts small, but expands to become a comfortable home for the lord of the manor. In the earliest days, windows are few, and small to make them easily defended. As the times become more peaceful, the walls are pierced by more and larger windows.

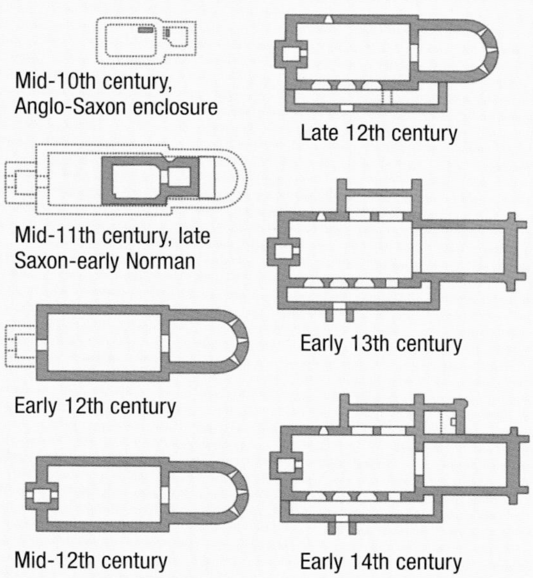

CHAPTER 2

# Life in the Castle

## An Early Feudal Castle

In the Dark Ages, the Roman fortifications were dismantled and their stones used for building houses and churches. When castles begin to appear again during the 9th and 10th centuries, they are constructed from wood.

The castle pictured here is typical of the earliest Norman fortifications. As the Normans conquer lands in northern France, England, and Italy, they need strongholds that can be erected quickly and defended against the hostile natives. Many of these wooden structures take the form known as the motte-and-bailey castle.

The motte, or mound, is surrounded by a fortified enclosure called a bailey. The bailey is protected by a ditch, the earth from which is thrown up to form a steep-sided bank. This raises the height an attacker must climb to reach the timber palisade that runs along the top of the bank. This "ring-work"—the term usually applied to a castle's outer defenses—is formed from stout tree trunks rammed into the earth and fixed together.

### The Norman-style castle

A wooden platform runs along inside the palisade to form a walkway, and the space below is sometimes filled in with earth to thicken the base of the palisade. Inside the ring-work stands the motte, usually about 15–30 feet high, sometimes surrounded by a second ring-work. The top of the mound is flattened and on its summit stands a tall wooden tower, called a keep or *donjon*.

Where the palisade is pierced by a gate, a second area of enclosed ground forms the bailey. Another ditch and palisade surrounds the bailey, and the two fortifications are connected by a wooden walkway or ramp.

The bailey contains a kitchen, barns, stores, stables, animal pens for livestock, workshops for carpenters and smiths, a chapel and a well, as well as domestic quarters for the lord's retainers and servants.

### Using the lie of the land

The exact layout of these motte-and-bailey castles varies considerably, depending on the features of the local terrain. For instance, an existing hill or rise in the ground might be used for the motte, otherwise it must be man-made. Some early castles have even been constructed inside the remains of pre-medieval earthworks, such as old Celtic hillforts, which provide additional outer rings of ditches and banks.

The Normans brought the motte-and-bailey castle to England, and many were erected within months of the country's subjection. However, most have now been rebuilt of stone to be far stronger.

If danger threatens, the local serfs and *villeins* take their goods and livestock to the castle for protection.

**1.** Wooden palisade standing on top of a rampart made from earth dug out of the ditch.

**2.** The castle's main gateway, with defensive extensions of the palisade on either side.

**3.** Bridge across the main defensive ditch, connecting the main gatehouse to the outer bailey.

**4.** The drawbridge can be raised to prevent attackers from reaching the secondary gatehouse in the palisade surrounding the outer bailey.

**5.** Outer bailey, with its several buildings for smiths, carpenters, stables, kitchens, and quarters for the servants and workers.

**6.** Outer bailey well, usually used only in times of siege.

**7.** The main ditch completely surrounds the entire castle inside the palisade.

**8.** Walkway over the cross-ditch, connecting the outer bailey to the inner bailey, with its own gatehouse.

**9.** Inner bailey, with lord's stables and armed retainers' quarters.

**10.** Raised motte.

**11.** The wooden *donjon* or castle keep stands on top of the motte. It only has small windows on the upper floor to make it easier to defend against attackers who might break through all the other defenses.

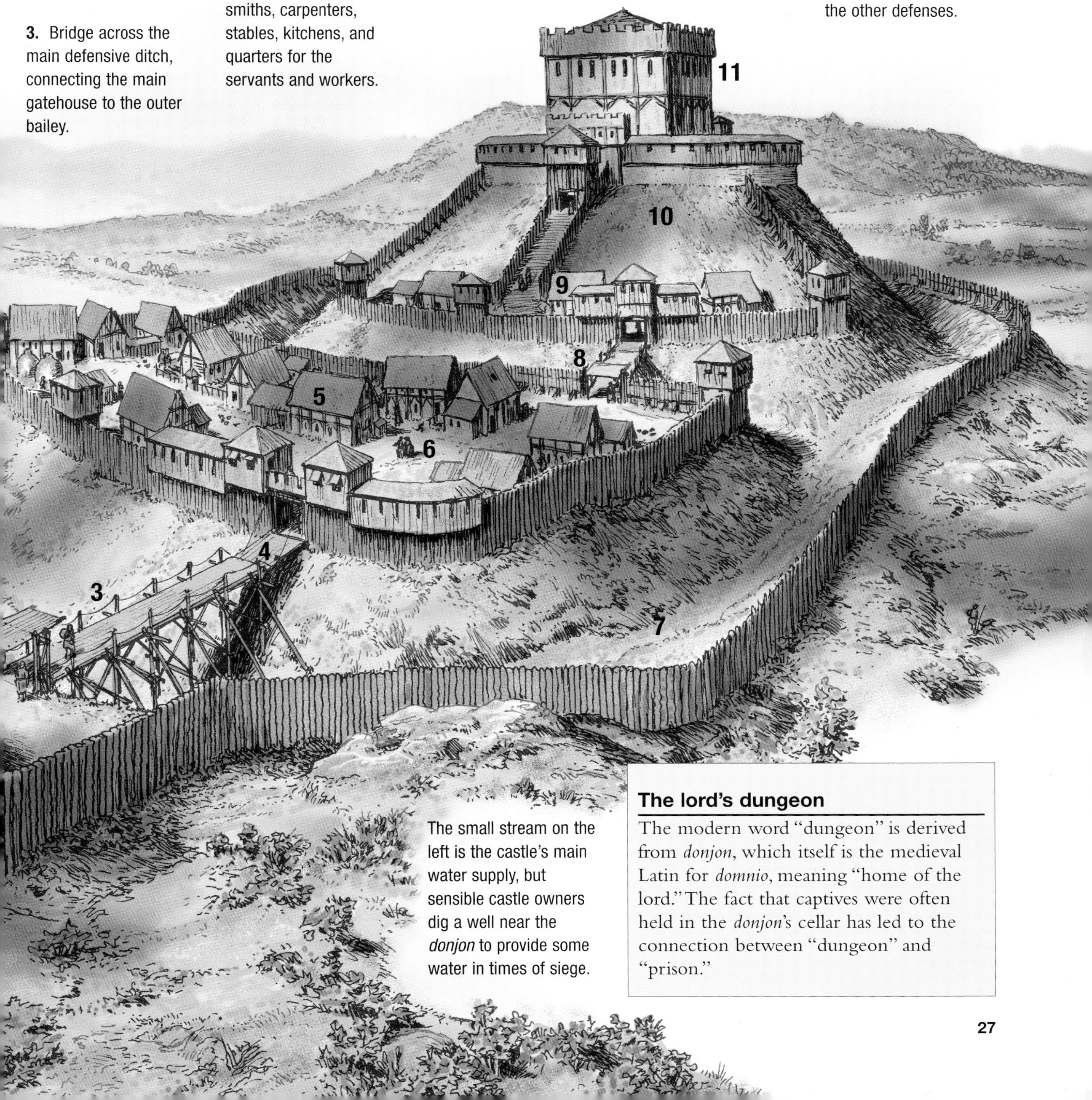


The small stream on the left is the castle's main water supply, but sensible castle owners dig a well near the *donjon* to provide some water in times of siege.

**The lord's dungeon**

The modern word "dungeon" is derived from *donjon*, which itself is the medieval Latin for *domnio*, meaning "home of the lord." The fact that captives were often held in the *donjon*'s cellar has led to the connection between "dungeon" and "prison."

# The Medieval Stone Castle

**Within a few years of the Norman conquest of England, Norman-French castles of stone have replaced the early wooden motte-and-bailey structures.**

Castles are centers for administration and the dispensation of justice. They are constructed at strategic sites, often along borders, roads, or rivers, or in a stretched line to enable easy communication with each other. Sometimes a site is chosen because its terrain is ideal or because the lord wishes to control an immediate area, perhaps following its seizure from another noble.

A single castle can command the countryside for a radius of about 10 miles, which represents a day's ride out and back. Invading armies usually prefer to avoid pitched battles, and so send soldiers to pillage, which destroys the local economy while at the same time feeding their own men.

But a garrison can also cut off the raiding enemy's supply lines and act as a base for massing troops for counterattack. This means that an invader cannot seize any land until he has captured its castles. Because sieges are expensive, castles therefore act as a deterrent to invasion.

Those regions that are most in dispute between nobles or kings always have the greater concentration of castles within their boundaries. There are several common types of castle, reflecting the needs of their owners, and the main purpose to which they are put.

## Tower keep—Conisbrough

This is an example of a tower keep, a castle where the *donjon* stands alone, without extensive outer ring-works. It was erected in about 1185–90, during the Third Crusade (1188–92) and the reign of King Richard I, by the half-brother of Richard's father, King Henry II. Its semi-circular bailey is little more than an entrance yard.

Conisbrough is one of the first circular keeps erected in Britain, and is unusual in having six wedge-shaped buttresses jutting out. Only the one that partly contains the chapel is not solid throughout the levels. There are four floors above a vaulted basement, with a first-floor entrance.

Typically, there are few windows, and they are mostly narrow arrow slits.

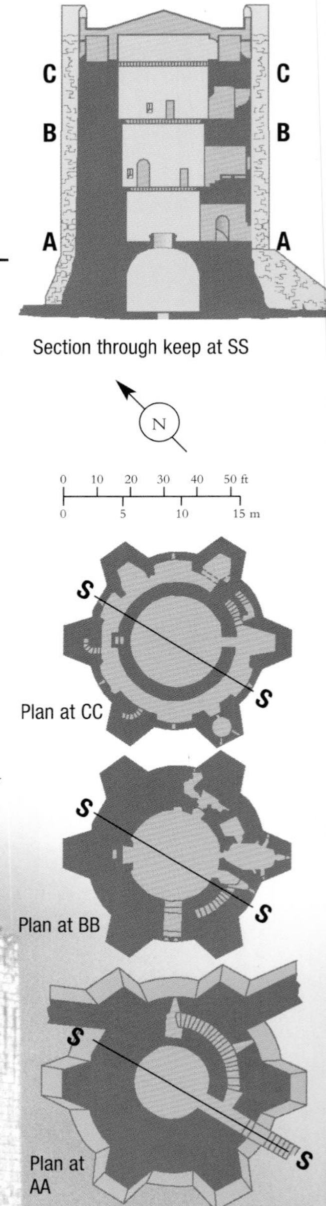


The circular *donjon* at Conisbrough has large buttresses, which show clearly on the section and floor plans.

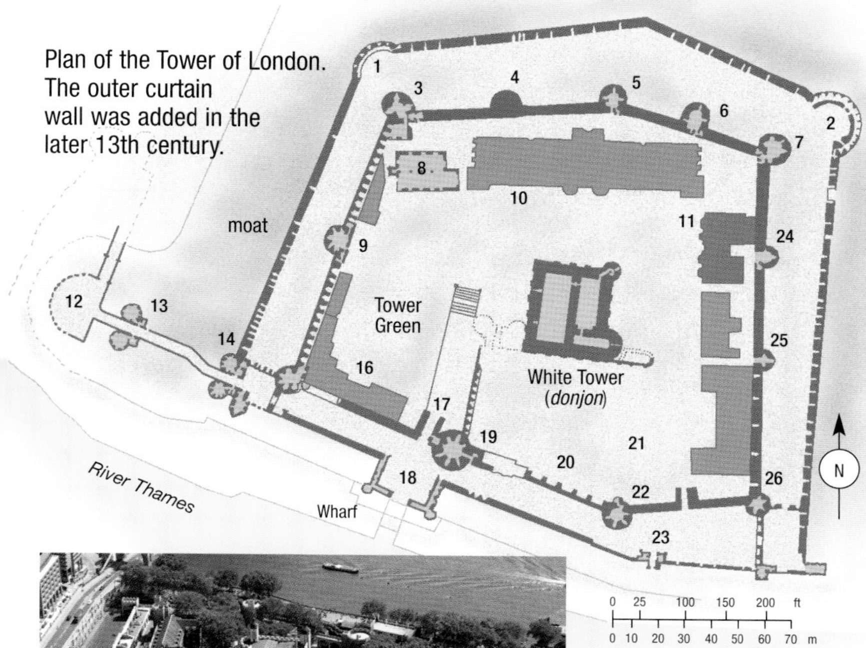


Plan of the Tower of London. The outer curtain wall was added in the later 13th century.

1 Legge's Mount
2 Brass mount
3 Devereux Tower
4 Flint Tower
5 Bowyer Tower
6 Brick Tower
7 Martin Tower
8 Chapel of St. Peter ad Vincula
9 Beauchamp Tower
10 Waterloo Barracks
11 Museum
12 Lion Tower
13 Middle Tower
14 Byward Tower
15 Bell Tower
16 Queen's House
17 Bloody Tower
18 St. Thomas's Tower
19 Wakefield Tower
20 Site of Great Hall
21 Roman town wall
22 Lanthorn Tower
23 Cradle Tower
24 Constable Tower
25 Broad Arrow Tower
26 Salt Tower
27 Well Tower

This aerial view clearly shows the Tower of London's concentric rings of defense.

## Concentric castle—Tower of London

William the Conqueror of Normandy began the castle in 1066. Within ten years, work started on the huge *donjon*, known as the White Tower, because of the whitewash used to protect it from the weather.

With King Edward I's moat, 160 feet wide, and an outer circuit of walls (1275–85), the Tower of London is one of the most powerful castles in Europe. It has housed the royal mint and the royal zoo.

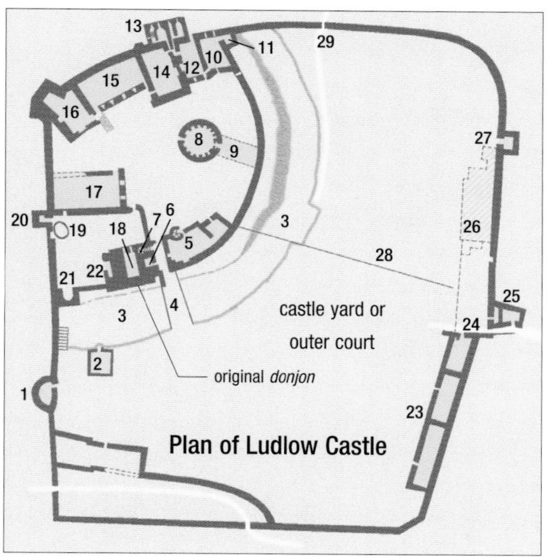


Plan of Ludlow Castle

1 Mortimer's Tower
2 Magazine / ice house
3 Moat
4 Bridge (originally a drawbridge)
5 Buildings of Sir Henry Sydney
6 Porter's lodge
7 Staircase to keep
8 Norman chapel
9 Site of chapel choir
10 Apartments occupied by sons of Edward IV
11 General room
12 Armory
13 Watch tower
14 State apartments
15 Council room
16 Prince Arthur's Tower
17 Kitchens
18 Original chapel, later a prison
19 Well (85 feet deep)
20 Lion's Den Tower
21 Norman Tower
22 The 'Black Hole'
23 Stables
24 Main gateway
25 Offices (fire watch)
26 Barracks
27 Beacon Tower
28 Iron palisades across outer court
29 Sallyport

## Curtain wall castle—Ludlow

In a curtain wall castle, the wooden palisades enclosing baileys are replaced by stone walls—the "curtain." Some do not have a keep and make up for the lack of a great tower by making the single ring of defensive curtain wall as impressive as possible. The walls have strong mural (wall) towers that jut out, allowing archers inside to shoot along the wall face at attackers.

Ludlow castle, sited near the Welsh border, is one of a line of Norman castles built to pacify the countryside and hold back the unconquered Welsh. Begun around 1085, the inner bailey is separated by a rock-cut ditch and protected by a curtain wall.

**Above:** Ludlow's unusual circular Norman chapel sits in the inner bailey. The *donjon*, one of the first stone-built keeps in England, was originally the gatehouse on the early curtain walls around the inner bailey.

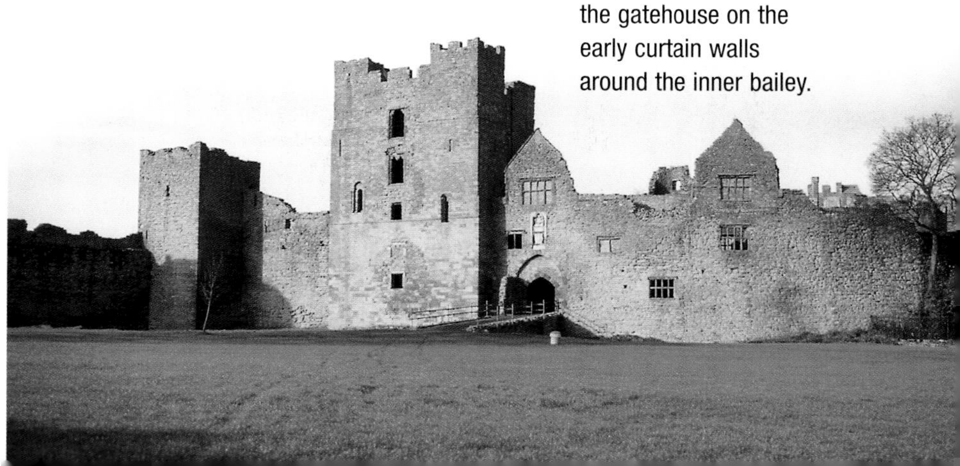

# A Castle Under Siege

Open conflict—expensive in men and horses—is avoided whenever possible. But if a lord shelters in his castle, the invaders must inevitably lay siege to it. Attackers have tools and tactics to employ… and defenders have their countermeasures.

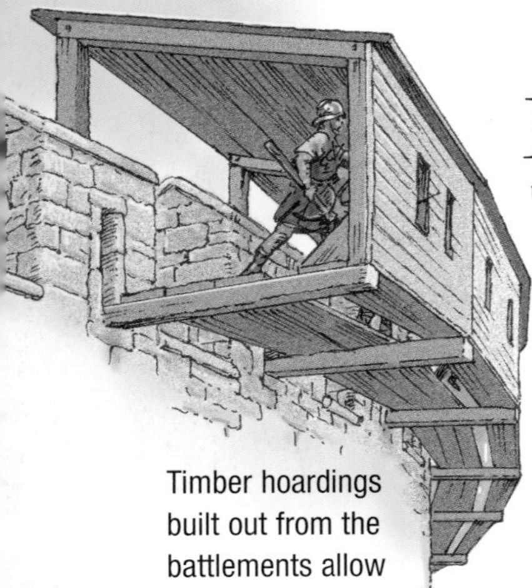

Timber hoardings built out from the battlements allow defenders to stand in front of the wall face and fire down at attackers through slots in the floor.

Easier options to a possibly bloody assault are usually exercised first. Surrounding the castle and starving the garrison into surrender sometimes works. Bribes can bring a lord's castles into the hands of another noble. If these tactics fail, the use of sheer terror by physical demonstration before the walls of a fortress—with the assistance of captives or the heads of slain opponents—can be enough to persuade defenders to give up.

## Taking a castle

Fortresses are attacked in several ways. One of the most effective is to dig a mine underneath the walls for the attackers to emerge inside the castle. More commonly, the mine is dug under a wall or tower and wooden props used to shore it up as it is dug. Smeared with fat and set alight, the props collapse and bring down the wall.

The defenders set out bowls of water and watch for telltale signs of vibration, but

**Above:** Machicolated parapets are formed by projecting the battlements forward and supporting them on stone corbels, creating slots between them for dropping offensive material.

**Below:** The torsion catapult's twisted ropes fling up a throwing arm inserted into them to release a missile.

**Above:** The ballista's bow arm shoots a large bolt. The screw is used to wind the slider back when the bowstring is engaged on the trigger.

**Right:** The trebuchet has a throwing arm swung up by pulling down the other end with ropes or, as here, a box filled with earth or stones.

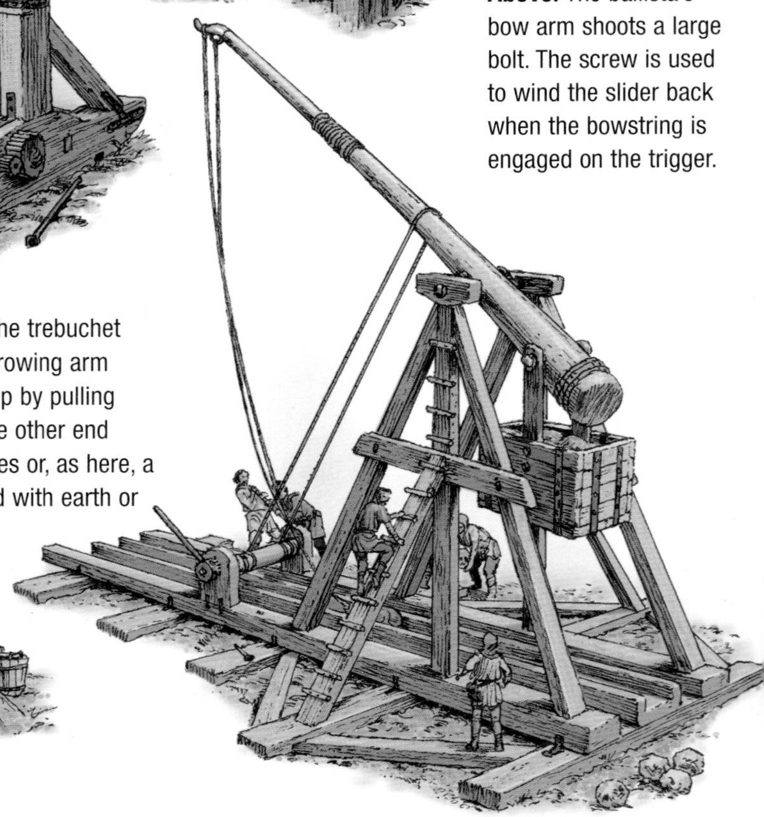

mines are very difficult to stop. Effective measures include digging a countermine to break into the enemy workings, or erecting a makeshift palisade built behind the threatened wall. A moat filled with water is the best deterrent to mining.

Sometimes a trench is dug up to the walls, protected with timbers, so men with picks can prize stones from the wall. Battering rams and drills are used to dig into it. These are countered by lowering sack cloth to deaden the blows. Rams shelter under sheds covered with wet hides to protect against fire arrows and other combustible materials thrown down from the walls.

The medieval armory is comprised of several engines for hurling rocks and large arrows. If a direct assault is required, the simplest means are ladders, but this is extremely hazardous—the defenders try to push ladders away with forked poles, and assailants can only arrive singly at the wall-top.

Far more powerful is the siege tower, or belfry. Huge wooden structures higher than the battlements act like gantries. Wheeled up to the walls, men in larger groups can attack the defenders. There might be a ram or shed at the tower's base or a catapult at the top. Cumbersome and vulnerable to fire, towers too are covered in hides. Sometimes they sink into hidden pits the defenders dig under the cover of night.

**A castle under attack**

A battering ram, slung under a mobile shed, is hitting the wall, where defenders have lowered a pad to muffle the blows. They also hurl down barrels of burning oil, but wet hides help to dampen down the flames. Some attackers scale ladders, but arriving at the top singly, they are easily beaten back. A mobile siege tower has been moved over a specially built causeway of earth and stones across the ditch.

Soldiers attack across the tower's lowered drawbridge, and a catapult on the top level shoots large stones into the castle.

# Building a Castle

The construction of a castle requires planning and the gathering of numbers of men and materials. But the first task is to choose a suitable site.

Selection of a castle's site is the lord's decision, advised by his senior knights and his architect—usually the master stonemason. Wherever possible, natural features of the landscape are used to their advantage, such as hilltops, cliffs, or mountain crags. A rock foundation is always best, for it deters enemies from mining underneath. Rivers not only offer the opportunity of a moat, again deterring mining, they are also a lifeline during sieges and an obstacle to enemies in themselves. If there is good pasture or woodland nearby, even better.

Architectural or engineering plans for castles are rare and the masons simply work from their own measurements. Freemasons are put to work cutting squared ashlar, moldings, and stone tracery. Roughmasons lay the stone, while layers build walls and hewers work in the quarries.

The construction requires a long list of other workers—miners, hodmen (stone carriers), carpenters, woodcutters, hammerers, levelers, foundation workers, well-diggers, fencing workers, lime-burners (for making mortar), mortar-makers, porters, smiths, plasterers, glassmakers, ditchers, carters, carriers, barrow-men, water-carriers, and pickaxe-men. On a large castle there might be as many as 3,000 workmen.

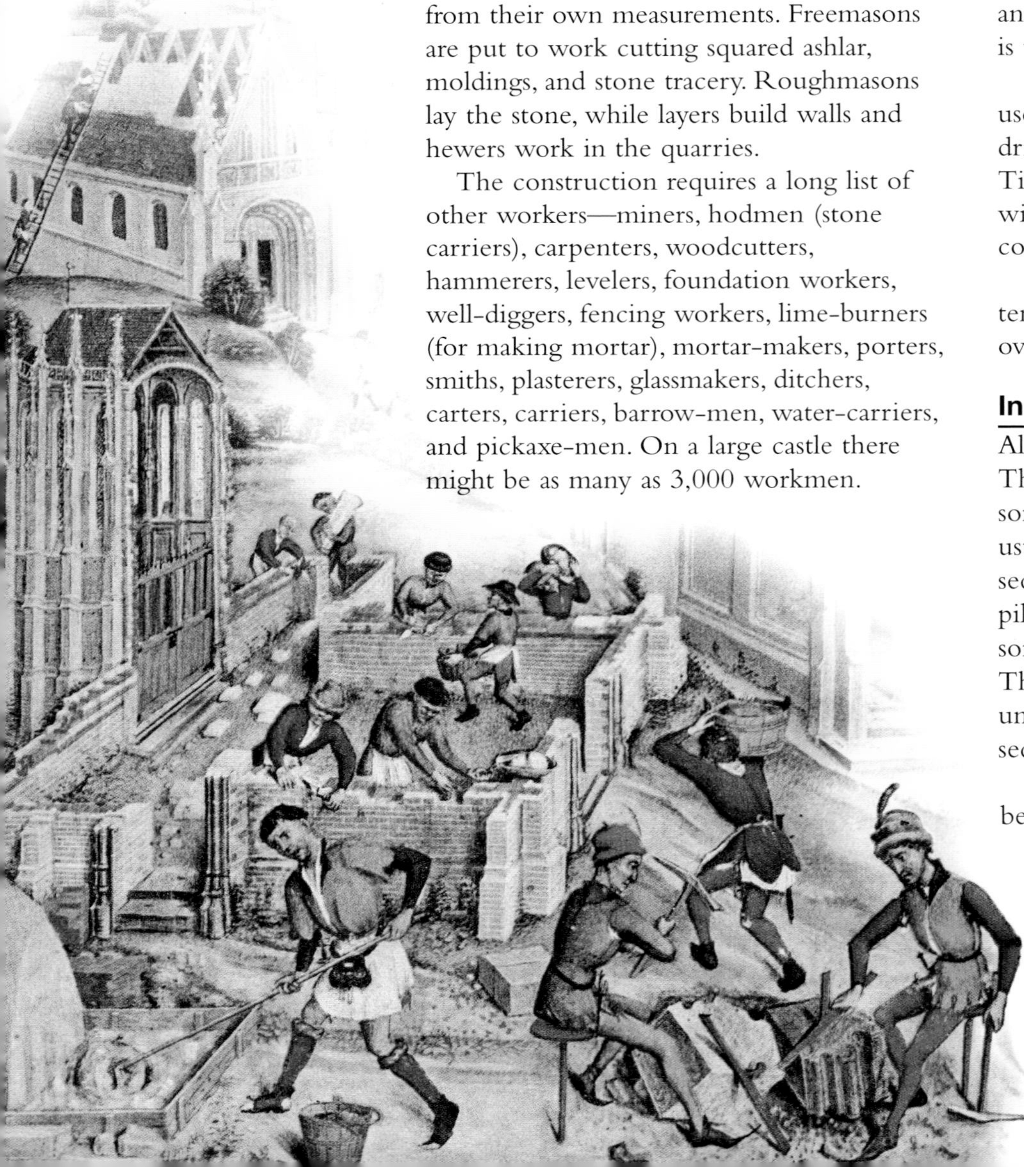

**Below:** Builders of the 14th century at work. In the foreground, two masons prepare stone using T-squares, ruler, and adzes, while a laborer mixes a load of lime mortar.

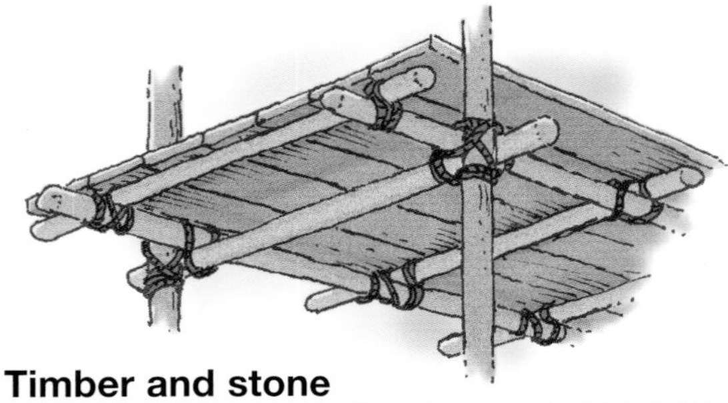

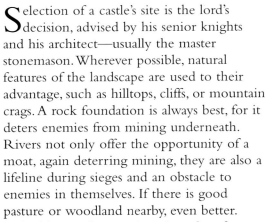

## Timber and stone

The carpenters are kept busy because wood is used everywhere. Shuttering for molding concrete, roofs, beams, and flooring, doors, window shutters, and room paneling—all are made from wood. So is the scaffolding. Holes in the walls, called putlog holes, are left for the insertion of scaffolding beams and below battlements for wooden hoarding.

The castle's defensive walls, towers, and the keep are constructed with rubble faced with dressed stone, or ashlar. The bonding mortar is made from sand, lime, and water, the lime is sometimes prepared on-site by burning limestone. Iron is needed for nails and tools, some of which are of steel. Plaster is used for interiors.

Workmen's tools differ little from those in use today. A block-and-tackle or a treadmill-driven windlass hoists stone and timber. Timber piles are driven into the ground with a ram, or a raft of timbers is constructed on soft ground.

A large castle could take between two and ten years to build, and often was extended over the centuries.

## Inside the keep

All castles have one basic element—the hall. This is a large room with a lofty ceiling, sometimes on the first floor, but more usually raised to the second story for greater security. Rows of wooden posts or stone pillars support the timber roof, although some later castles have vaulted stone ceilings. The windows are typically small and unglazed, equipped with wooden shutters secured by iron bars.

In a first-floor hall the floor is simply beaten earth, with a stone or plaster covering. Second-story halls have a timber floor, supported by wooden pillars or stone vaulting in the basement below. Floors are strewn with rushes sprinkled with sweet-smelling herbs. Although the rushes are replaced at intervals and the floor swept, the rushes often smell badly. One chronicler observes that under them lies "an ancient collection of beer, grease, fragments, bones, spittle, excrement of dogs and cats, and everything that is nasty."

The lord and lady's chamber is called the solar. Its principal item of furniture is a great bed with a heavy wooden frame and springs made of interlaced ropes or strips of leather, overlaid with a feather mattress, sheets, quilts, fur coverlets, and pillows. The bed is designed for dismantling so it can be taken along on the frequent trips a lord makes to his other manors. Linen hangings curtain off the bed, which can be closed at night for privacy as well as protection from drafts.

Chests for garments, a few "perches" or wooden pegs for clothes, and stools make up the remainder of the furnishings. Sometimes a small anteroom called the wardrobe adjoins the chamber—a storeroom for cloth, jewels, spices, and plates, and where the lady's dressmaking is done.

## Home in a tower

**1.** The tower houses the spiral stairs to all floors.

**2.** An overhanging wooden defensive gallery.

**3.** Quarters for men-at-arms and servants.

**4.** The lord and lady's private quarters. Behind the curtain is their latrine (**5**), which empties into the moat below.

**6.** Centerpiece of the keep is the great hall, where important guests are welcomed and main meals are taken.

**7.** The entrance hall.

**8.** A large kitchen provides all food.

**9.** Provisions are stored deep in the cellars of the tower. This is where the vital water-well is.

**10.** The dank dungeon.

**Above:** Forms of timber scaffolding used by castle builders. Horizontal beams are inserted into "putlog" holes left in the walls by stonemasons.

# Jobs in the Castle

In medieval society there are two classes—people with status, and those with none. While the lord and members of his entourage may have status, to function they need the support of the many laborers and peasants.

The first impression of a castle is of the lord and his knights and men-at-arms riding helter-skelter over the drawbridge and under the portcullis of the gateway, but beneath them a startling number of skilled craftsmen and laborers inhabit the various structures around the baileys.

Among those with status, the three most important functionaries are the steward, marshal, and bailiff. The steward, or *seneschal*, is responsible for the manor's estates and the castle's domestic administration. He directs the household servants and supervises events in the great hall.

The marshal is in charge of the household's horses and wagons, as well as acting as the transportation captain. Under him work the farriers, grooms, carters, blacksmiths, and clerks. Farriers shoe horses, while grooms feed and care for the horses.

Carters bring wood and stone to the castle. Blacksmiths forge and sharpen tools and weapons, maintain armor, and make all the metal items needed, such as door hinges and defensive window grills. Clerks keep the accounts, pay the wages, and are responsible for checking goods in and out.

The bailiff supervises the manor's serfs and peasants, He allots them jobs and ensures that they have the right tools for the job. When a tool breaks or becomes blunt, he organizes the blacksmiths to repair or sharpen it. He also supervises any building repairs.

## The domestics

Attached to the functions of the kitchens, and reporting to the steward, the butler cares for the lord's cellar. He is in charge of the large *butts* (barrels) and *little butts* (bottles) of wine, cider, and ale. The butler also has a large staff under him, consisting of brewers, tapsters (those who "tap" the large butts to draw off the liquor), and cupbearers, who serve the drink.

The bottler runs the milkmaids and butter churners in the "bottlery," or buttery. In the kitchens, there are several cooks working under instruction from the head cook, while the lowliest workers, called scullions, scour and wash the dirty pots, pans, and the lord's fine pewter, silver or gold plates. There are many other people involved in keeping the lord's table supplied—bakers, poulterers, fruiterers, and slaughterers.

Chamber maids look after the private apartments and while ladies-in-waiting attend to the lady's personal needs, the lord has several young page boys at his command. These are usually of noble birth, sent from their homes and given into his care until they are old enough to become squires.

The role of minstrels should not be overlooked. While playing musical instruments and singing ballads provides entertainment, roving minstrels also act as news-bearers and—through learning the old stories as part of their ballads—they are the historians of the Middle Ages.

While the aristocrats enjoy their leisure (here on a hunt in the spring), an army of lowly workers keeps a castle in working order.

## Other medieval jobs

This list suggests how many tasks need to be fulfilled in and around a castle.

**almoner** (ensures the poor receive alms); **atilliator** (crossbow maker); **barber** (also acts as a surgeon, dentist, and blood-letter); **board-hewer** (joist and floorboard carpenter); **carders** (worker who brushes cloth after weaving); **dyer**; **ewerer** (brings heated water for the nobles' baths); **haywards** (gardener who tends hedges); **laundresses**; **messengers**; **musicians**; **spinsters** (women who spin yarn for cloth); **tanners** (workers who cure leather); **soap makers**; **candle makers**; **painters**; **plasterers**; **weavers**.

# The Noble Family

Ownership of land, either by force or as the king's gift, is what sets a noble apart from other lesser men. For the lord of a manor, the question of receiving land and assets from his father and passing them onto his son is an important one.

Wealthy lords have calendar books created for them, called Books of Hours, beautifully illustrated with scenes representing the months of the year. This is a scene from a French book made for the Duc de Berry.

**Above right:** While an eldest son can expect to inherit his father's estates and position, younger sons have little alternative but to become a page and then squire with another lord, become a monk, or take holy orders and become a priest. Some young men prefer to take up arms and join a crusade to recover the Holy Land from the Muslims.

The estates of an earl, a count, a baron, or a distinguished knight are his by the right of the king, but a good marriage settlement can add considerably to his holdings. It is technically impossible for women to inherit land (although there are notable exceptions to this rule), but on their marriage, the father will endower her, either with money or by giving her new husband access to some of his land as a holding. In principle, this should be returned to the lord if the married daughter dies or is divorced by her husband—but many small-scale wars have occurred when the husband refuses to return it.

## The problems of inheritance

Of course, on his death, the lord wants to hand on all his assets to his son to keep everything in the family. If he has no sons, the family property passes to the closest relatives, particularly surviving brothers. But in a noble family where there are several sons, life can become difficult. It is normal for the eldest son to inherit all his father's estates, which leaves his younger brothers with few options.

At the age of seven, a younger brother might be sent to serve as a page in another noble's castle (*see page 40*), and may never see his home again. When he is in his early 20s, if a second son is lucky enough to make a good marriage, he might receive land from his father-in-law, effectively becoming his feudal knight.

Many second and third sons seek a patron, a powerful noble who will take them into his retinue, where they can seek their fortunes as warriors, probably overseas by warring in France or in the Crusades. For sons who cannot inherit, the only other option is to take holy orders and become a churchman.

As for the daughters, failure to find a suitable husband—or, more likely, have one found for them—will almost certainly result in their being sent away to become a nun in a convent.

## The lord and lady's banquet

The noble family usually eats three meals a day. A small breakfast of bread and cheese at sunrise is followed in the late morning or about noon by the main meal of two to three courses. These consist mainly of meats and pastries, bread, wine, or ale, fruits, cheeses, and nuts. Since they are considered more as common fare for peasants, vegetables do not figure much in a noble's meal.

Before sunset a light supper is served of a meat stew, bread, and cheese, accompanied by song and music played by minstrels. A wandering troubadour might entertain with some yarns, and acrobats or contortionists are a popular diversion.

When a lord is in residence, he is frequently obliged to entertain traveling guests, other nobles, high-level clergy, perhaps even the king, all of whom are accompanied by their extensive retinues. The feast is the centerpiece of the entertainment and a great contrast to the everyday meals.

The guests can look forward to consuming quantities of beef, mutton, poultry, game birds, pork, venison (in season), fish, eggs of all kinds—everything presented in a variety of ways—cheeses, bread, and all washed down with gallons of wine, ale, cider, and mead.

**Above:** Unlike the serfs and peasants, nobles have some leisure time. Hunting with falcons is a favorite recreation.

**Center left:** Eating implements. Forks are almost unknown (although used in Italy during the 15th century, they only reach northern Europe in the 1600s). Most food is eaten by cutting and spearing it on a dagger, or a special dining knife. Spoons are so precious that they are made to fold up for carrying around.

**Right:** A minstrel and a jester.

## The big blow-out

Some feasts are truly vast in scope. In 1467, the Archbishop of York fed 6,000 guests on: 104 roasted oxen, 6 bulls, 1,000 sheep, 304 calves, 2,000 pigs, 1,000 capon chickens, 400 swans, 104 peacocks, 2,000 geese, 1,500 deer, more than 13,000 other birds (such as starlings, vultures, seagulls, herons, storks, cormorants, and cranes), 1,500 venison pies, 608 pikes, 12 porpoises and seals, finished with 13,000 bowls of jello, cold baked tarts, custards, and spiced fruits. In addition, a large quantity of alcoholic drink was consumed.

# Men-at-Arms

**When a peasant family has too many sons to support, there is little choice for the uneducated boys but to seek service in the armed retinue of their lord or one of his lesser knights. The more adventurous might look to a mercenary life.**

For men-at-arms, guarding castle walls and gatehouse duties are tedious. Trudging along as protective escorts for an important person can be quite difficult.

The number of military personnel defending a castle varies enormously, depending on the size of the castle. Three knights and ten men-at-arms represents a very small garrison. At the other end of the scale a royal castle might have as many as 100 men-at-arms, 20 or more knights, and a variety of lesser men, all serving under the constable. The constable is in charge of the retinue when the king or the noble lord is absent.

## A life on foot

A knight taking service is expected to come equipped with his own mounts, saddlery, weapons, and armor, but the peasant has no such resources and must look to his lord to supply his needs. This means he is never likely to have a horse and will go into battle on foot as an infantryman.

His level of protection and armament depends on the lord's financial status. Usually this is not a complete suit of armor, but comprises at least a helmet, a body defense in the form of a mail shirt, fabric armor, or a metal or leather breastplate, as well as a weapon such as a spear, pike, ax, or crossbow. Among the English armies, one of the most fearsome weapons is the Welsh longbow.

The lowliest level of men-at-arms are employed as security men in basic garrison duties. These include castle wall sentry duty, guard duty on the castle's gates, at the town gates, and the collecting of taxes from merchants entering or leaving the lord's domain. The more presentable man-at-arms may find himself in the retinue accompanying his lord when traveling, or seconded to the protection squad for a bishop journeying around his diocese.

## Bowmen

Those who show sufficient skill in their aim receive some training with the crossbow. This easily learned weapon fires a short arrow with sufficient power to injure or kill a knight in

French and English men-at-arms clash in one of the many battles of the Hundred Years War as France tries to take back land seized by the English crown.

plate armor at up to 200 yards. Crossbows are easier to aim than longbows because the crossbowman does not have to use a hand to hold the string back while aiming.

By contrast, learning to fire the longbow with skill takes a long time, and many longbowmen start their training as adolescents. The bow also takes great strength in the pulling arm to draw back the drawstring.

However, the longbow, because of its rapidity of fire, is a superior weapon to the crossbow, the machine gun of its age. An archer can shoot 10–12 arrows a minute across a range of up to 200 yards. Compared to this even the superior Genoese composite crossbow—made of wood, horn, sinew, and glue—is no match for the English weapon.

In a battle, when massed archers fire, their arrows fall from the sky with deadly accuracy like a hail storm, cutting down the enemy as a scythe reaps wheat.

## Soldiers for hire

With the *scutage* tax (see page 41), European kings are relying more and more on mercenary corps to supply fighting men for wars. The head of a mercenary band is called a captain, and it is his job to recruit skilled fighters, seek out contracts and levels of pay, and make sure his men receive their pay and agreed amounts of booty after a victory.

The majority of mercenaries are crossbowmen, although several gangs of English freebooters rove around Europe selling their services to the highest bidder who desires the power of the longbow in his army. The numerous small southern German states are the source of many mercenary bands, called *landsknechts*, and the same term is applied to Europe's most feared men-at-arms, the Swiss pikemen (*seen below*).

Switzerland's mountainous terrain supports fewer farms than anywhere else, which means the young men must move away as soldiers to earn a living. Their ferocious battles for freedom against the Habsburgs of Austria have taught the Swiss soldier all the skills needed to become the most professional mercenary in the business of warfare.

**Right:** A page spends most of his time riding horses and strengthening his body with exercises and wrestling. He learns how to fight with a lance, mounted on horseback, by "tilting" against a *quintain*. This is a heavy, human-shaped dummy with a shield hung on a wooden beam, which is free to swivel around a vertical pole. The page aims to hit the shield in its center. When hit, the *quintain* spins and agile riding is needed to avoid being struck by the returning dummy and falling from the horse.

# The Road to Chivalry

In medieval society, the best way for a man to gain advancement is to become a knight. It is not a way of life to which many are suited—the training is long and hard, but the successful attain high status, and possibly great wealth.

**Above:**
A knight is captured. Unlike men-at-arms, it is rare for knights to be killed in battle—they are worth more alive as captives, to be ransomed by their lord or relatives in return for their freedom.

The knightly code of chivalry grew during the 12th century, when knights bearing the cross of Christ went to the Holy Land to protect pilgrims from the Muslim Saracens who attacked them. Chivalry, or *chevalerie* (which derives from *cheval*, the French word for horse) is the name given to the idealized qualities of knighthood—religious devotion, honesty, courtesy, and impeccable behavior toward women. Failure to adhere to the code can lead to public humiliation and loss of social status.

However, many young, landless knights go on crusade in the East, which is considered to be a holy undertaking. But in reality they hope to grab land for themselves as a reward from the prince in command and rapidly make themselves a fortune—they do not always stick to the code of chivalry.

## Training for knighthood

In a period when all education is run by priests and monks of the Church, the sons of knights are brought up according to the code of chivalry. To qualify as a knight, a boy is sent at the age of seven to serve as a page in a great lord's household. His new master becomes his feudal superior. As well as acting as his lord's servant, the page is put through his paces in swordsmanship and horse-riding. At the age of 14 he becomes a squire and does chores and runs errands for a particular knight in the lord's retinue.

Since skill and prowess in battle is the ultimate aim, in a well organized household the military training pages and squires undergo is intensive. When there are no battles to be fought, the jousting tournament is a celebration and test of a knight's skill (*see pages 42–43*).

## Becoming a knight

At the age of about 21, a squire who has shown his mettle may qualify as a knight and swears an oath of allegiance to his feudal lord and loyalty to the code of chivalry. His lord then presents him with a knightly sword.

## A knight's military service

His military duties involve a certain period of service each year, and a knight is expected to be prepared to serve at all times. This involves attending his lord in person, equipped with a lavish kit of horse, armor, and weapons—although wealthier knights are often required to bring a retinue of foot soldiers or cavalry as well.

Military duty is usually restricted to set periods of six or eight weeks. If service beyond this is required, the knights are paid for their time. A knight who owns land, serfs, and tenant peasants can avoid direct military duty. With sufficient revenues from his fiefs, he can pay a tax called *scutage* (from the Latin *scutum*, a shield). This money is used by his overlord for the hire of experienced mercenary knights and infantry.

Pages and squires also receive some education. The chaplain—or more likely local monks—teach rudimentary reading and writing, some Latin and French. It is the lady's responsibility to oversee the young men's education in the courtly skills of manners and dancing, and how to behave in the king's court.

For about seven years from the age of 14 a squire attends his knight. His duties include dressing the knight in the morning, serving his meals, caring for the knight's horse, and cleaning his armor and weapons.

In return for his oath, the knight is guaranteed a secure place within the power pyramid of the feudal system. If he proves his prowess in battle, his lord might grant him a fief. In this way a knight becomes a landholder in his own right, and may pass the estate on to his elder son through inheritance. Younger sons either take service with other knights of ranking or enter the Church—there is no option of going into a trade.

## The dubbing ceremony

On the evening before the ceremony, the squire—let's call him Rolf—is ritually cleansed in a bath of rose water, and then stays all night in prayer alone in the local church. At dawn the priest hears the squire's confession before taking Mass. The ceremony takes place in front of family, nobility, and a congregation of well-wishers. The priest consecrates the blade with which Rolf will be dubbed a knight. *"Bless this sword, that thy servant may henceforward defend churches, widows, orphans, and all those who serve God, against the cruelty of heretics and infidels. . . ."* Rolf then kneels before his lord, who taps him lightly on each shoulder with the sword and proclaims him a knight with the words "Arise Sir Rolf." In addition to his sword, Rolf is presented with spurs, which are attached to his heels. With this, the new knight raises his sword to acknowledge the honor before returning it to its scabbard.

# Jousting—the Sport of Knights

Jousts are a great spectacle for everyone. They give superiors a chance to assess the fitness and skills of knights, who sharpen their fighting abilities and show off their courage—especially to the admiring ladies.

In the past, tournaments were a bloody business. The loss of life among the participants was so great that the Church forbade the burial of those killed in tournaments, claiming that "Those who fall in tourneys will go to Hell."

The first written rules governing the sport were written in 1066 by a Frenchman named Geoffroi de Purelli (who was killed in the very first tournament held under his rules). It is now customary for the knights to use blunted weapons and obey the stricter rules that were established in 1292, in the three types of tournament.

### The Mêlée

Also called the "tourney proper," this is the form of sport evolved from the brutal battles of the early days. It involves several knights contesting as every man for himself. At the sound of a trumpet call, they all charge into the arena and attempt to unhorse each other until the last mounted knight is declared the winner. Cheating—where several knights gang up on an individual—is common, although as soon as their victim is unhorsed the survivors turn on each other again.

### The Joust

Jousting is a contest between two individuals armed with lances, who ride toward each other on either side of a low, central partition. The rules are simple. A knight scores points for making a clean strike with his lance on the center, or "boss," of his opponent's shield. More points are scored if the opponent's lance is shattered or if he is unhorsed by the strike. A combatant is automatically disqualified if he strikes either his opponent or his opponent's horse anywhere on the body.

Although the lances are round-ended wooden weapons, injury to the jousters is common. The central divider is a measure to reduce injury to the horses—considered much more valuable than the men.

A European knight mounted on his destrier, or warhorse, goes into battle during the Crusades.

### The knight's warhorse

In war and at the tournament, a knight rides a very powerful, highly spirited warhorse called a *dextrarius* or destrier. The name comes from the way the knight's squire leads the horse—since he always walks on the left side of the horse's head, he holds the animal with his right hand, and *dexter* is the Latin for right.

Destriers are so expensive for knights to purchase that many lords offer them instead of pay. Their replacement cost is the reason they are protected from harm during jousting contests.

When preparing for a mounted charge in battle, the knight rides to the front on a palfrey. This is a lighter, short-legged, long-bodied horse that walks at a gentle amble and is also suitable for women to ride. In this way, his destrier is allowed the maximum time to rest before the heavily armored knight mounts, ready for the charge. In either case, the squire is responsible for looking after the spare horse for his master.

**Above:** Two combatants in the joust meet on the "field of honor."

**Center:** A knight prepares for a tournament and receives his "insignia" from his lady love.

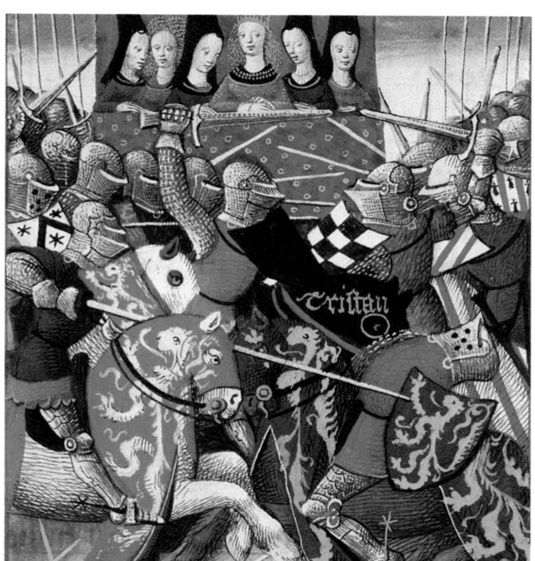

**Right:** A medieval illustration shows knights ganging up in a mêlée. The beautiful ladies of the court watch and argue among themselves over whether the knight carrying their "honor" will win.

## The Practice tournament

Rather more of a sideshow, there is little ceremony and there are few rules in a Practice tournament. The two main events are riding at a quintain (*see page 40*) or "riding at the rings," in which the knight charges at a ring suspended on a cord and attempts to carry it off on the tip of his lance.

## The code of honor

Winning knights are awarded customary "golden rings" along with kisses in a formal and elaborate prize-giving ceremony by the ladies of the court, who are central to the whole ideal of knighthood. Chivalrous and romantic conduct are important aspects of the tournament.

A combatant knight selects a beautiful lady—preferably married to a husband of higher rank than his own, through which he might gain a future advantage. The lady gives the knight her "honor," a scarf perhaps, or maybe her handkerchief, for him to wear in the joust. If he fights successfully, the knight expects to receive his reward—a courtly kiss.

CHAPTER 3

# The Power of the Church

## Father of the Community

While the kings and powerful nobles might control, or even own, the lives of ordinary folk, they have no hold over a medieval person's soul—that is in the hands of the Church.

In many respects, the great churchmen wield as much power as any noble. Like the feudal system, the Roman Catholic Church has a complex hierarchy that orders the spiritual life of every person, and in many cases their daily toil.

The pope is head of the Church, God's representative on Earth. Among his many functions, the pope has the power to make a deceased person whose virtue and holiness has been proven into a saint, through the rite of canonization.

Beneath the pope, cardinals act as the pope's advisors. They take their name from *cardo*, the Latin for "hinge," which explains their function, ensuring that the pope's wishes are communicated throughout Christendom. It is from among the cardinals that a new pope is elected on the death of the previous one, and only cardinals may vote in the ballot.

Next in the chain of command come the archbisops, also known as metropolitans, archbishops are appointed by the pope to have authority over a wide territory of several dioceses—the territorial administrative units of the Church, also called sees or bishoprics.

**Right:** The Church's power is symbolized in the act of coronation, a ceremony during which archbishops crown a monarch, in this case King Henry II of Castile, Spain in 1369.

**Opposite:** Despite ordering the lives of nobles and commoners alike, there are times when people resent the Church's power. This manuscript illustration shows the pope, bishops, and clerics defending their "fortress of faith" against heretics and "unbelievers."

### The major orders

The **bishop** is the senior minister of the Church. He may ordain lesser ministers and confirm people who have been baptized by a priest. His area of authority is called a diocese. Bishops are granted a *cathedra* or throne to sit on, and so their church buildings are called cathedrals. Bishops are supported by one or more **archdeacons**, who have the authority to administer a part of the diocese for the bishop. In turn, an archdeacon is senior to the **dean**, the cleric who is put in charge of the care and repair of a cathedral.

A **priest** is the ordained minister of the Church. He can give the Holy Sacrament to his congregation at mass, baptize newborn infants, marry people, hear confessions, and hand out punishments called penances. He can also grant God's forgiveness or absolution for sins committed. Priests may give a final blessing to the dying—this is called extreme unction. Priests are usually appointed by a bishop to care for a local community called a parish. Beneath the priest comes the **deacon**, a cleric with a special responsibility for the collection and distribution of alms—

charity for the poor of the parish. His assistant is called a **sub-deacon**, the lowest of the major orders and a stepping stone to promotion within the Church hierarchy.

## The minor orders

Highest of the minor orders is that of the **acolyte**, who has responsibility for a church or cathedral's candles and assists the priest in preparations for mass.

In the next rank, **exorcists** are responsible for the casting out of evil from people possessed by Satan and his demons. This exorcism, as it is called, uses prayer and special incantations to expel the spirits.

In the third rank comes the **reader**, also called the **lector** from the Latin word meaning *to read*. His principal responsibility is to conduct readings of the Bible during services. The lowliest cleric is the **doorkeeper**, whose functions are to head processions and look after the fabric of a church's building.

# The Abiding Faith

Even among the aristocracy, few people are able to write or read. Only those who enter the ministry of the Church receive any education. As a result, the monasteries and great cathedrals are the main centers of learning.

Even if a peasant were capable of reading the Bible, he would not understand a word of it, for it is written in Latin. While a noble lord might understand some of the spoken Latin, very few peasants can. This means that senior priests and clerics are the only interpreters of God's word.

In the parish of Ludford, almost everyone attends the Sunday services, and punishments are handed out to those who fail to show up, and to the "slug-a-beds" who arrive late.

As usual, the priest thunders from his pulpit, delivering a blistering sermon on the nature of mankind's evil. Few of his parishioners are in any doubt as to the dreadful fate that awaits them in the afterlife if they sin (*see page 57*) because he explains in graphic detail the horrors of Hell.

## Everyone is a sinner

Confessing sins to a priest and making atonement through a punishment, or penance, is essential if the person is not to accumulate so much evil that they will be sent to Hell at the end of their lives. Sins are graded in evilness and divided between two different forms.

Mortal sins—those that directly offend God—are hard to pardon, while venial sins—acts that offend against other people—are graded according to their severity. Those who die unrepentant of a mortal sin will certainly go straight to Hell for all eternity, but the majority of venial sinners who die before paying for their sins are sent to purgatory, where they are cleansed through suffering before their admission to Heaven.

Sins also have a second form. A sin of commission is a wrong act and a sin of omission is not doing something that should be done. Even "wrong thoughts" are considered to be sinful. In return for the priest offering God's forgiveness through absolution, the sinner must accept a punishment or penance.

## Punishment for sinning

A penance might be as mild as being made to help clean up the churchyard, but it could be as severe as spending a whole day going without food, painfully

**Far left:** Sunday sermons can carry on too long for simple peasant folk, who soon lose track of what their priest is trying to tell them.

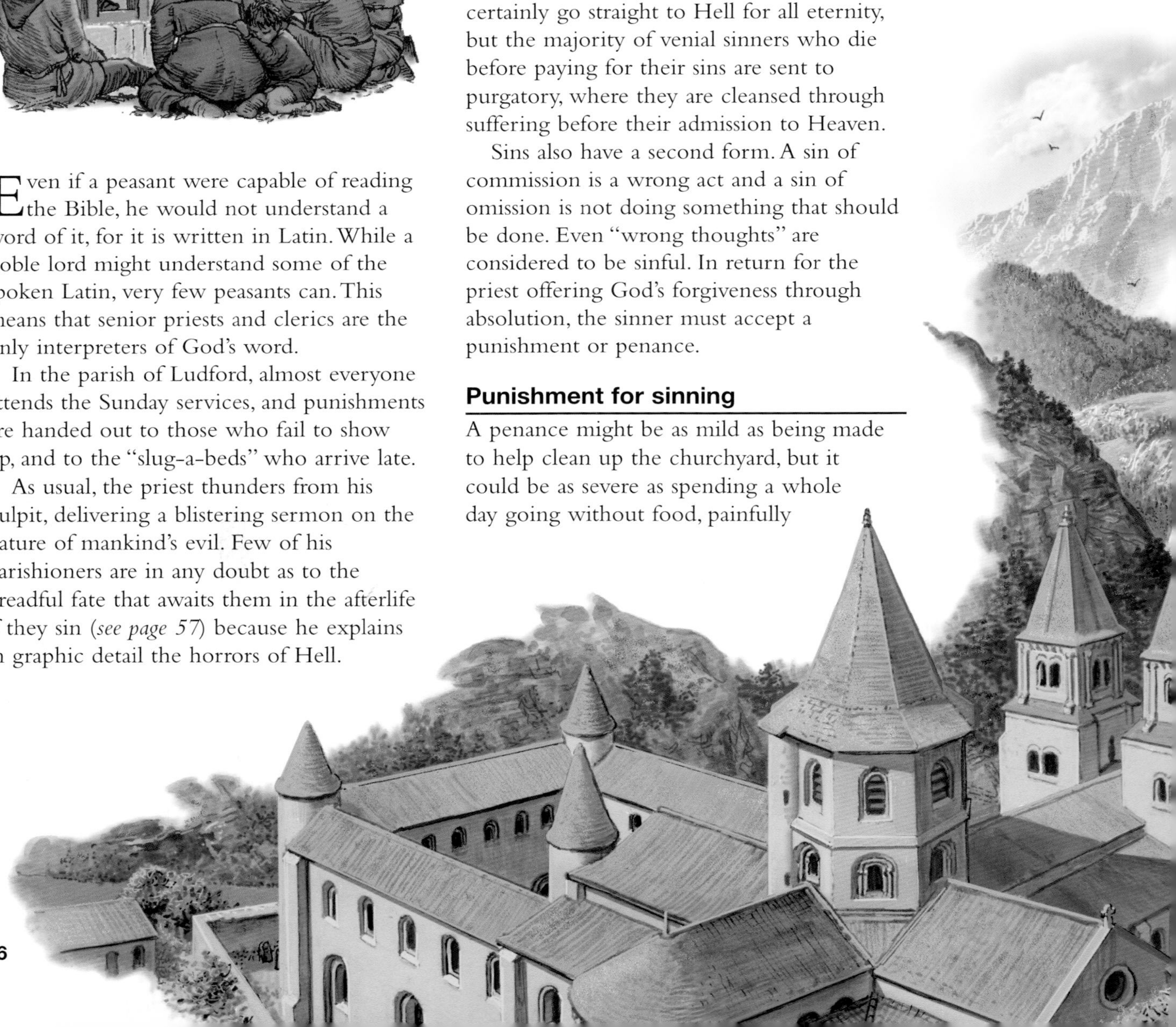

kneeling or lying prostrate on the cold, hard, stone floor of a church in prayer.

Nobles, too, must do penance for their sins, although to avoid the humiliation of a punishment witnessed by commoners, the wealthy lord is more likely to make atonement by paying for a new chapel or making a grant of money to a religious order.

## Pilgrims' progress

A popular form of penance is to go on a pilgrimage to visit a holy shrine. The object of the pilgrim's veneration may be the tomb of a saint, a place noted for miracles of healing, or a gem-studded box called a reliquary, containing a piece of the True Cross of Christ, or the bone or personal possession of a saint—a "relic." Although simony, the trade in religious artifacts, is outlawed, such is their power that it remains a big business, and objects said to possess fabulous powers are being uncovered all over Europe.

For some, a pilgrimage might mean little more than a day's walking to enjoy the company of others on an important day, but others take the journey more seriously as a form of atonement for some terrible sin they committed. Still others make it a way of life, journeying from shrine to shrine in a way of life similar to that of a monk or hermit.

There are many small holy shrines, but the three great places of western Christianity are Rome, Compostela, and Canterbury. In Rome, pilgrims can visit many holy sites including the burial places of the Apostles and many other martyrs. A prayer offered to St. Vitus will result in a third of a lifetime's sins being pardoned, while the pilgrim who looks on the handkerchief of St. Veronica—which bears the imprint of Christ's face—can wipe out up to 3,000 years of purgatory.

## The Church's indulgence

There is another way to cut down the time a soul might have to spend in purgatory, by buying an "indulgence." An indulgence offers the recipient the extra chance to pay his debt while alive, usually in the form of giving a part of his wealth to the Church treasury.

Unfortunately, this has led to numerous "professional pardoners" selling indulgences on a large scale for their own profit—a practice which will surely send themselves into the despair of purgatory one day.

## Seeking sanctuary

Through the rules of sanctuary, the Roman Catholic Church offers a safe refuge for those fleeing from justice or persecution. Any who seek refuge within the precincts of a church building designated as sanctuary may remain there for 30 to 40 days. When the time has expired, they are allowed to go into exile without harm. Violation of sanctuary is punishable by excommunication.

In some cases, there is a stone seat within a church, called the frith-stool, on which the seeker of sanctuary has to sit in order to establish his claim to protection. More commonly, there is a large ring-knocker on the church door, the grasping of which gives the right of asylum.

Archbishop of Canterbury, Thomas Becket, is assassinated in the cathedral by knights of King Henry II in 1170. Later made a saint, his tomb has made Canterbury one of Christendom's great pilgrimage centers.

**Below:** Pilgrims on a road in southern Europe are relieved to at last see the shrine that is the object of their long and weary journey.

# Prayer and Toil—the Monastery

At its best, the monastery represents the core of medieval Christian culture. Places of prayer and religious contemplation, monasteries are also farms, craft centers, libraries, colleges, and hospitals.

Above: Monks devote themselves to a life of religious contemplation, but the hours spent in prayer after a long day's work can send even the most devout to sleep in the church pews.

There are several different orders of monastic houses, with varying rules, but the basis of their way of life follows the ideals of St. Benedict. He founded the first western monastery at Cassino, Italy, in 529. Monks devote their whole life to God and retire inside the monastery precincts under vows of poverty, chastity, and unquestioning obedience to a superior.

## A monk's day

Life in a monastery is organized around an unchanging cycle in which attending divine service occupies at least five out of every 24 hours. The bell rings out at midnight in summer, in some orders two hours later during the winter, summoning the monks to Matins (from the Latin word for morning). This service lasts about an hour, after which they can return to sleeping until 6 a.m., when it is time to return to the church for the half-hour service called Prime.

**Left:** The contemplative life in monasteries has led to an outpouring of religious literary work. Books are painstakingly copied out by hand. Here Eadwine the Scribe works on a psalter (book of prayer).

A brief breakfast of homemade bread and ale gives the sustenance needed for work or study. Many monks toil in the monastery fields, often aided in heavier tasks by the village serfs offering work instead of the obligatory church tithe (*see page 15*). Some monks, skilled in writing and art, copy out sacred texts in the library and illustrate them, while others tend to livestock, the cooking, and the sick and elderly infirm.

Work ceases at 9 a.m. for Mass, after which matters of monastery business are discussed in the monks' chapter house before a second Mass at 11 a.m. This is followed at midday by the main meal of soup, bread, vegetables, fruit, and cheese taken in the dining room, called the refectory.

Although meat is available, it is forbidden on certain days of the year, called fast days, and since fasting days take up almost half of the year, meat is not often eaten. As they take their meals, the monks listen in silence to readings from the Scriptures.

After the meal, rest is allowed until 2 p.m., when the service of Nones (the commencement of the ninth hour of the day) is held. This is followed by further work until 6 p.m.—broken by Vespers (from the Latin for evening) at 4 p.m.—when a light supper is served in the refectory, followed by the day's last service of Compline at 7 p.m. Shortly after its completion, the monks retire to their dormitory to sleep, still dressed in their habits.

While peasants struggle to keep warm in the harsh winter, some monks live a life of comparative comfort.

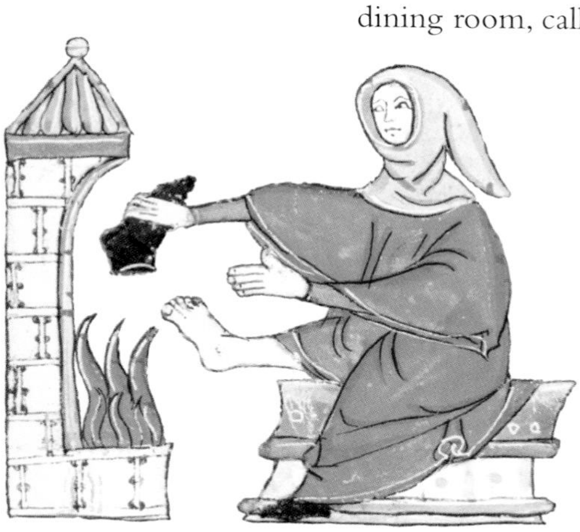

## An ordered life

The superior of a monastery or an abbey is called the abbot. The abbot is supported by his next in command, the prior. Below these two are the "obedientaries," monks with specific duties. The most senior obedientaries are shown in this "family tree."

Abbot
Prior

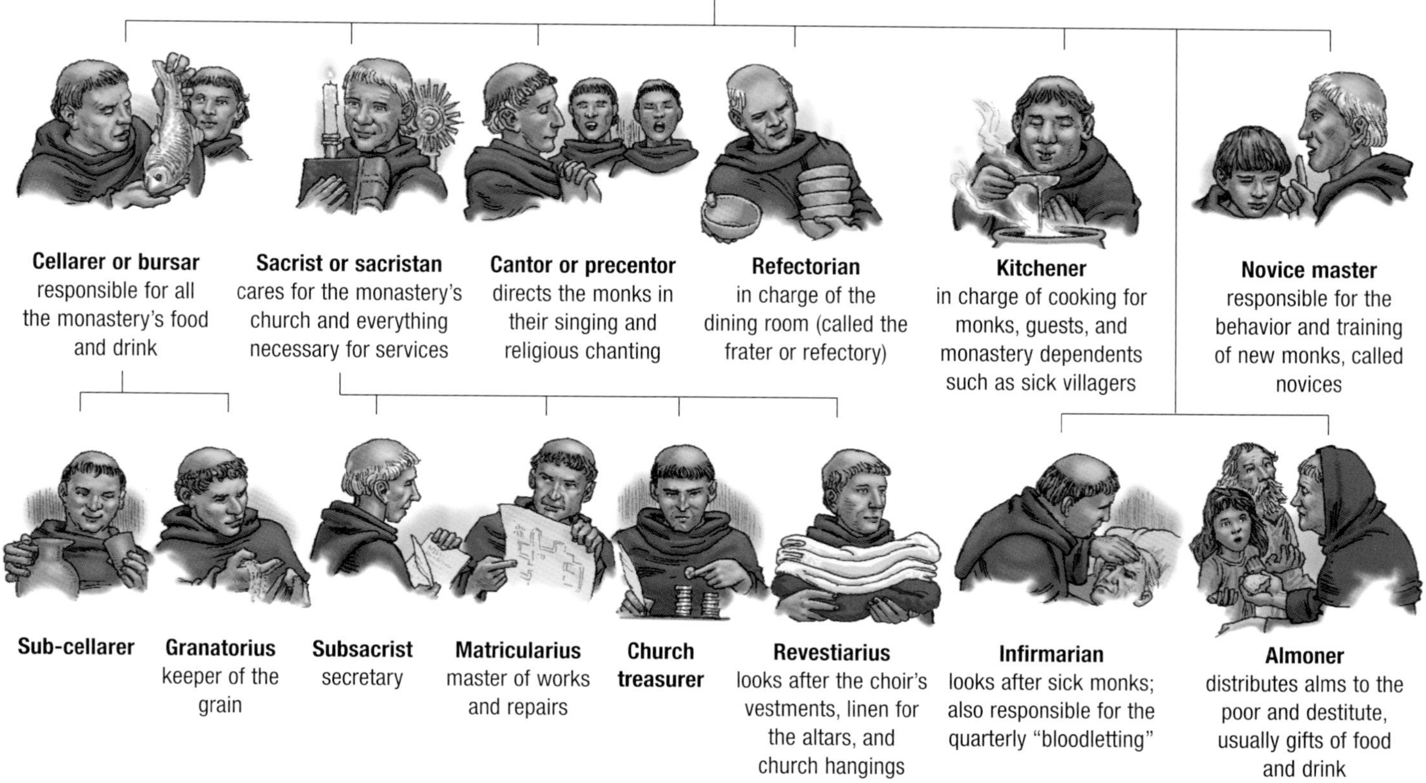
**Cellarer or bursar**
responsible for all the monastery's food and drink
**Sacrist or sacristan**
cares for the monastery's church and everything necessary for services
**Cantor or precentor**
directs the monks in their singing and religious chanting
**Refectorian**
in charge of the dining room (called the frater or refectory)
**Kitchener**
in charge of cooking for monks, guests, and monastery dependents such as sick villagers
**Novice master**
responsible for the behavior and training of new monks, called novices
**Sub-cellarer**
**Granatorius**
keeper of the grain
**Subsacrist**
secretary
**Matricularius**
master of works and repairs
**Church treasurer**
**Revestiarius**
looks after the choir's vestments, linen for the altars, and church hangings
**Infirmarian**
looks after sick monks; also responsible for the quarterly "bloodletting"
**Almoner**
distributes alms to the poor and destitute, usually gifts of food and drink

# The Monastery as a Surgery

Medieval medicine is practiced by few people—for most commoners, their local barber is also the doctor-surgeon—but it is in the monastery that the most scientific care for the sick is found.

The churchgoer—which means everyone—learns daily of how Jesus performed miracles of healing, and stories abound of saints and their relics performing similar miracles. In its notion of Christ's blood curing people's sins, Christianity is a "healing" faith. So it is natural that monks should adopt the role of healers and pharmacists.

St. Benedict, who founded the Benedictine Order of monks, advised his brothers "before all things and above all things care is to be had of the sick…and let the sick themselves remember that they are served for the honor of God." The monks believe that a healthy body means a healthy soul and that failing to take care of the soul is a sin against God.

To achieve a healthy body (and a healthy soul), the monastic healer has a variety of methods at his disposal.

## The herb garden

In their role as librarians, the monks have access to numerous and often ancient works of herbal medicine; the herb garden is an important part of any monastery. Depending on the region and the climate, as many as 120 herbs are grown. Some of these have known medicinal properties, others are believed to have a magical effect (*see "Wealth in horseradish"*).

The common thistle and a large relative of it called butterbur are commonly cultivated in monasteries and, used in combination, are an effective remedy against the plague. There are herbs to heal just about every ailment, from bad dreams to insect stings, snakebites to stomach complaints, from skin wounds and broken bones to mouth cancers. Garlic is commonly added to other herbs since, in addition to its healing properties, it wards off evil spirits, witches, vampires, and snakes.

Mixed with various types of oil, wax, and even animal dung, herbs are taken orally or applied as poultices to wounds.

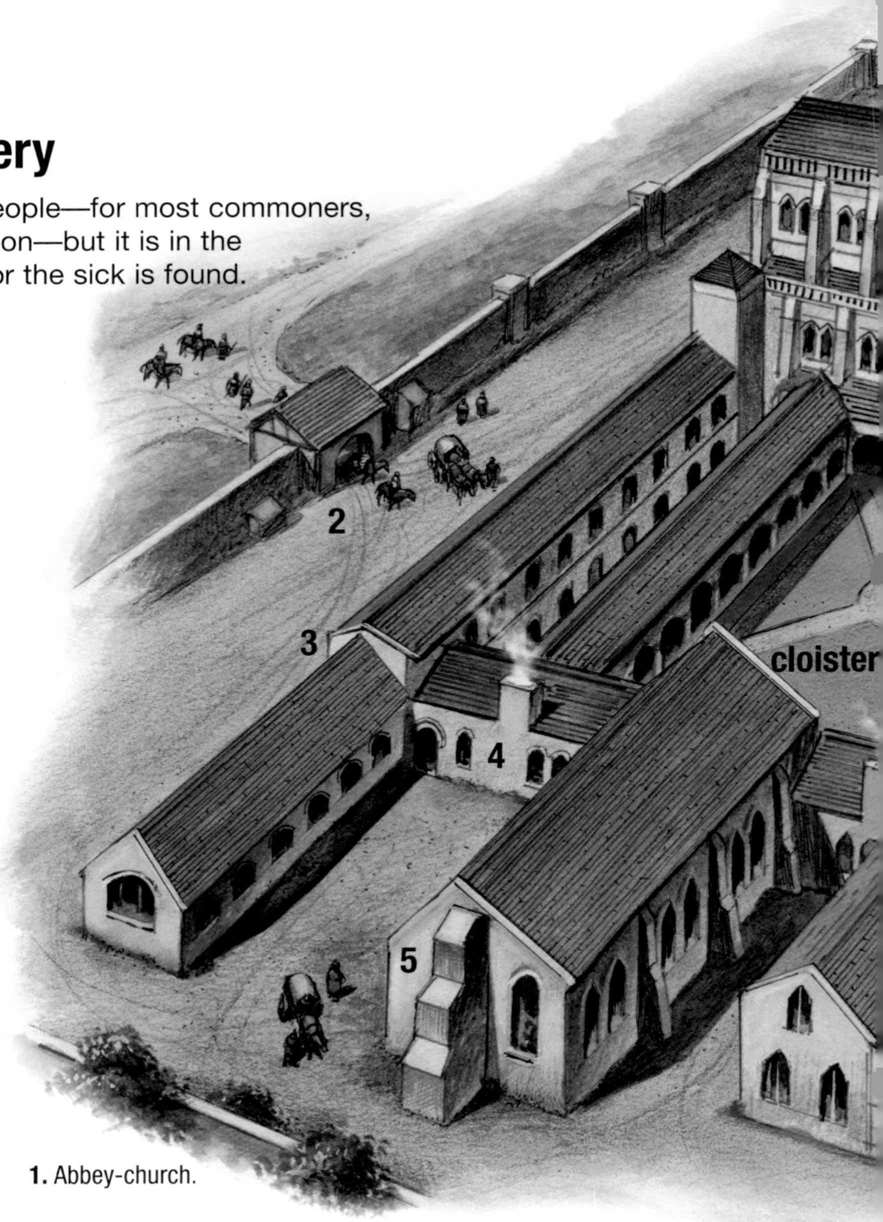


**1.** Abbey-church.

**2.** Gatehouse, manned by a porter.

**3.** Monks' dormitories.

**4.** Kitchens, with pantry, bottlery, and cellar.

**5.** Refectory (dining room).

**6.** Abbot's quarters.

**7.** Infirmary for care of sick and elderly monks.

**8.** Herb garden with herbarium.

**9.** Fish ponds.

Although herbs are gathered all through the year, harvest is the busiest time. The plants are cut and tied in bunches to hang in the herbarium to dry. It is a place thick with the strong, aromatic smell of recently cut herbs. Although in many cases fresh herbs are more effective, dried plants help to cure the sick right through a harsh winter.

## Bloodletting

It has been known for centuries—even as far back as the ancient Greeks—that a person's blood contains four elements, or "humors" (from the Latin *umorem*, meaning fluids). These are black bile, phlegm, blood, and yellow bile, and they are associated with the four elements that make up everything in the universe—earth, water, fire, and air.

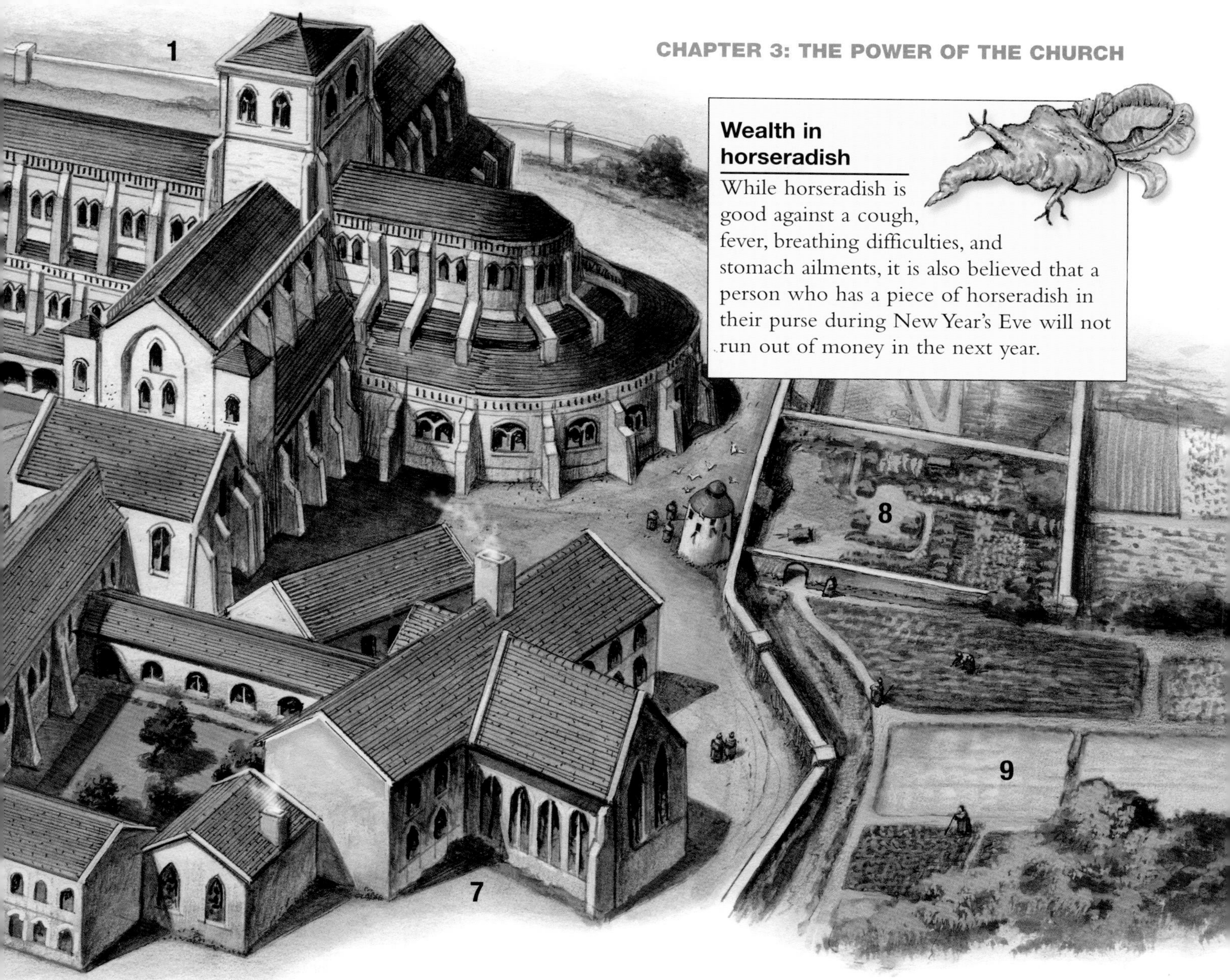


### Wealth in horseradish

While horseradish is good against a cough, fever, breathing difficulties, and stomach ailments, it is also believed that a person who has a piece of horseradish in their purse during New Year's Eve will not run out of money in the next year.

The four elements must remain in balance for a person to be healthy, so any illness is blamed on an excess of one humor or another. For instance, a fever has hot, dry symptoms, due to an excess of yellow bile. The remedy is to drain the excess by bleeding the patient. An alternative might be to prescribe an icy bath which, being cold and wet, will stimulate yellow bile's opposite humor, phlegm.

There are three methods of bloodletting: leeching, venesection, and cupping. Leeching involves attaching to the patient a blood-sucking worm known as a leech (from *laece*, the Anglo-Saxon word for doctor). The leech draws off a large quantity of blood, and in extreme cases several are attached to the patient to speed up the process.

In venesection a vein is slit open and the blood allowed to flow into a bowl. Cupping involves the application of heated glass cups over the skin. They create vacuums that draw blood up through the skin.

Whichever method is used, the purpose is the same: to reduce the excess blood in the body and so restore balance and health. In a monastery, bloodletting is considered necessary on a regular basis, at least four time a year, more frequently in times of general ill health. Many communities even have a special building for bloodletting, which is overseen by the infirmarian.

Once a monk has been bled, he is relieved of his labors for a period of time and is not even expected to attend services. The monastery's infirmary beds are often filled with monks recovering from the loss of blood, happy in the knowledge that they are healthier than before.

### Fact Box

The medieval notion of "humors" still remains in our vocabulary today when a happy person is said to be in "good humor" and a bad-tempered person is called "ill humored."

# Building God's House

All over Europe, the new wealth created by the growth of towns is expressed through the building of cathedrals, great abbeys, and churches.

Such is the frenzy of religious construction that a contemporary chronicler claims the land "is clothed in a white robe of churches." In the Middle Ages there are two architectural styles of church building. The first, used between 950 and the mid-11th century, is called Romanesque, because of its adoption of Roman ideas like the rounded arch, seen in the few remaining ancient ruins.

The second—a development of Romanesque—began with the building of the abbey church of St. Denis, Paris, in 1132 and soon spread all over Europe. This is called Gothic (*see pages 54–55*).

**Above:** This French church has a classic Romanesque barrel-vault roof.

## Adoption of the Roman basilica

The classic form of the large late-Roman church is the *basilica*, essentially a long rectangular building consisting of a central *nave*, flanked by one or more *aisles*. In a basilican church the nave and the aisles are separated by a row of large columns, which support the roof over the nave.

If there are two aisles on either side of the nave, a secondary line of columns separates the flanking aisles. In most cases the aisles are covered by a lower roof, while the nave's walls soar above them and are pierced by windows. This upper area, or *clerestory*, lets light into the building.

The rounded arch is the basic element of Romanesque style.

### A cruciform basilica

This is the floor plan of Durham Cathedral.

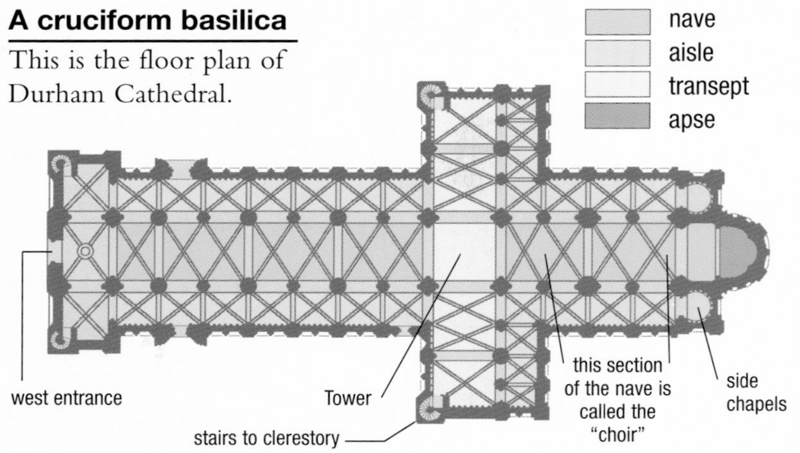


At the eastern end of the nave, a semi-circular area—the *apse*—houses the altar. In some cases, the apse is distanced from the nave and the side aisles by a rectangular area called the *transept*, which runs at right angles to the nave. In many later churches, the transept exceeds the width of the main building to create a "cruciform" basilica—the shape of a cross.

## Romanesque style

The basic element of Romanesque is the rounded arch (*seen left*), a style borrowed from the ancient Romans. These arches rest on massive masonry piers.

The first Romanesque basilicas were constructed with an arcade of arches along either side of the nave and a flat or A-frame wooden roof. Later examples have a taller nave under a "barrel vault." In this case, transverse arches are built across the nave, supported on the columns of the side arcade. The gaps between are filled with wedge-shaped bricks to form the vault.

However, an arched roof creates its own problems. The nave walls must be immensely thick to support the lateral pressure of the roof, which is trying to push the walls outward, and ideally, there should be no clerestory windows to weaken the walls.

**Above:** The nave and roof of Ely Cathedral and, **below**, a simplified cutaway shows the basic structure of a Romanesque basilica like Ely.

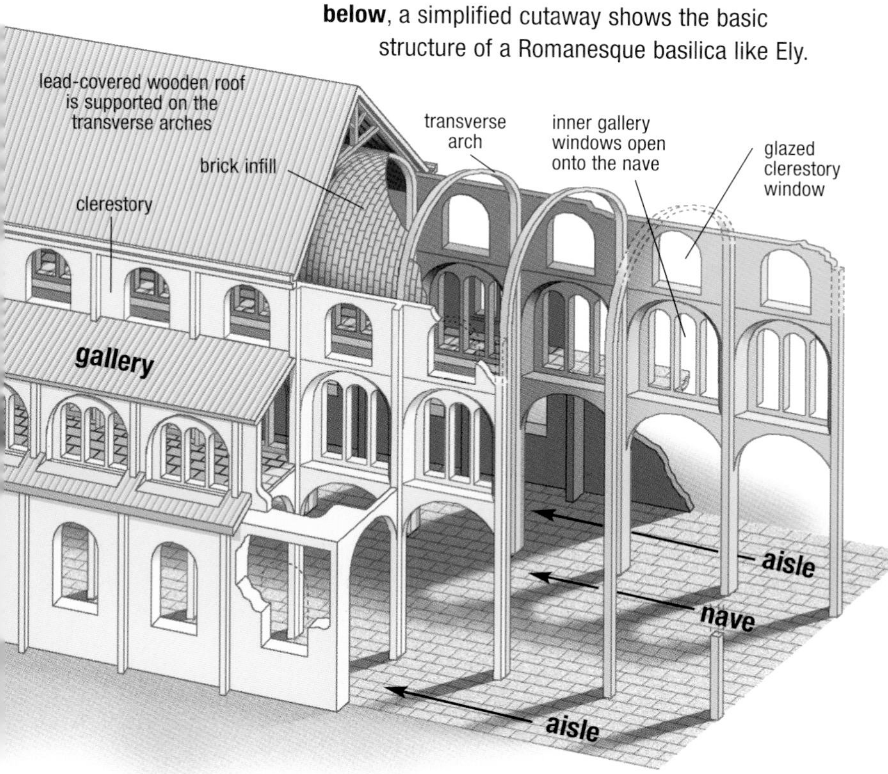

**Above:** The next step in Romanesque's architectural development is the vault, with rounded diagonal ribs but pointed transverse arches.

Churches built like this are usually very gloomy inside.

To get around this design fault, architects have strengthened nave columns and then linked them by diagonal arches that run along the vaulted nave like a series of ribs. This is called "groin vaulting," and the system adds sufficient strength to the structure that clerestory windows can be added. This rib-vaulting is the basis of the

# Gothic—Reaching for Heaven

The greatest monuments to Christendom in the Middle Ages are the soaring cathedrals and churches built in the Gothic style, which started in Paris in 1132, and whose spires now tower above every city and town.

The pointed arch defines the Gothic style.

In a Romanesque church, with its boxes of rounded arches, the walls bear much of the weight-load of the vault and roof.

The innovations of the Gothic style are the ribbed vault and pointed arch. In a Romanesque church the vault is ribbed from side to side, dividing the roof into a number of regular bays. The addition of two diagonal ribs make a sturdy framework that allows the triangular sections between the ribs to be made of lighter stonework.

However, because the diagonal ribs are longer than the crossing (transverse) ribs but still need to be a half-circle, their crossing point is higher than the top of the transverse and arcade arches. This spoils the clean lines of the Romanesque style because the central roof line has to change heights to match the different heights of the arches. The solution is to make the transverse arches pointed at the top so that they are the same height as the transverse ribs.

## Freeing the form

In the next development, architects made all the arches pointed so that nave and transverse arches have become the same height, bringing back the clean lines of the Romanesque. This so-called Gothic style has many advantages over Romanesque. The shape of the arches means that the strain on the piers is transferred from the horizontal axis to the vertical. This allows designers to reduce the size of the support columns while raising the height of the vault.

It is important to provide extra reinforcement to the piers at the point where they support the pointed ribs. The final Gothic innovation is the flying buttress; a heavy stone pier built outside the cathedral. Arches spread from these, over the low roofs of the cathedral aisles to reinforce the piers of the nave at the maximum point of stress. Secondary arches sometimes support the walls of the aisles.

**Left:** This cross section through the choir of a Gothic cathedral built between 1344 and 1351 shows how a flying buttress supports the upper nave wall.

**Right:** The vault of Gloucester Cathedral shows how the addition of many pointed rib-arches can become a magnificent and decorative fan of umbrella-like spokes.

With the weight of the building resting on a highly engineered structure of ribs, piers, and buttresses, the walls no longer bear any load, so they can be pierced with many windows. This has led to the introduction of stained-glass windows, filling cathedrals with magnificently colored light. In some examples it seems as though the very walls of the church are made of glowing glass.

The result is a light, airy structure, filled with a soaring sense of grace, where spiritualism is allowed free rein. The sheer height of the vault leads the worshippers' eyes toward Heaven, while the marching arcade of tall arches running the long nave focuses attention on the apse and altar in the far distance.

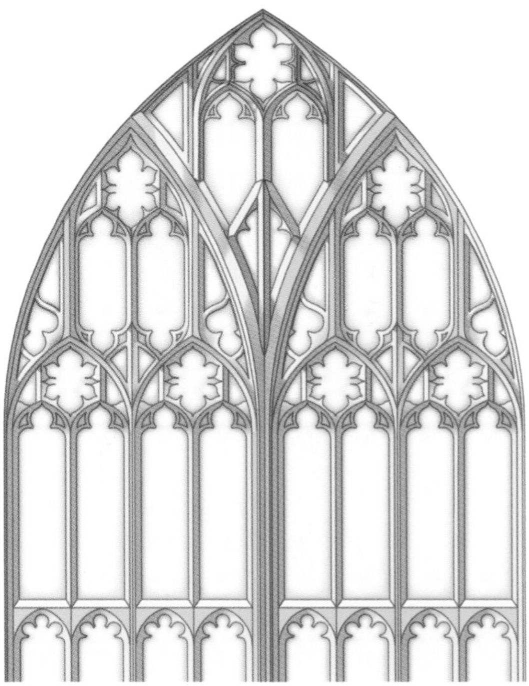

**Above:** Lincoln Cathedral, built between 1192 and 1280, represents a perfect form of early Gothic.

The stonemasons' art reaches its peak with a style of Gothic called Perpendicular because of the repetition of vertical elements. The stone tracery of windows is so delicate as to be breathtaking. This example is from the south transept of Gloucester Cathedral, c.1335.

# Pestilence—the Black Death

The Black Death has been the worst human disaster in Europe's history. It began in the fall of 1347, when seamen returning from Kaffa on the Black Sea arrived in Sicily aboard Genoese ships suffering from a strange disease.

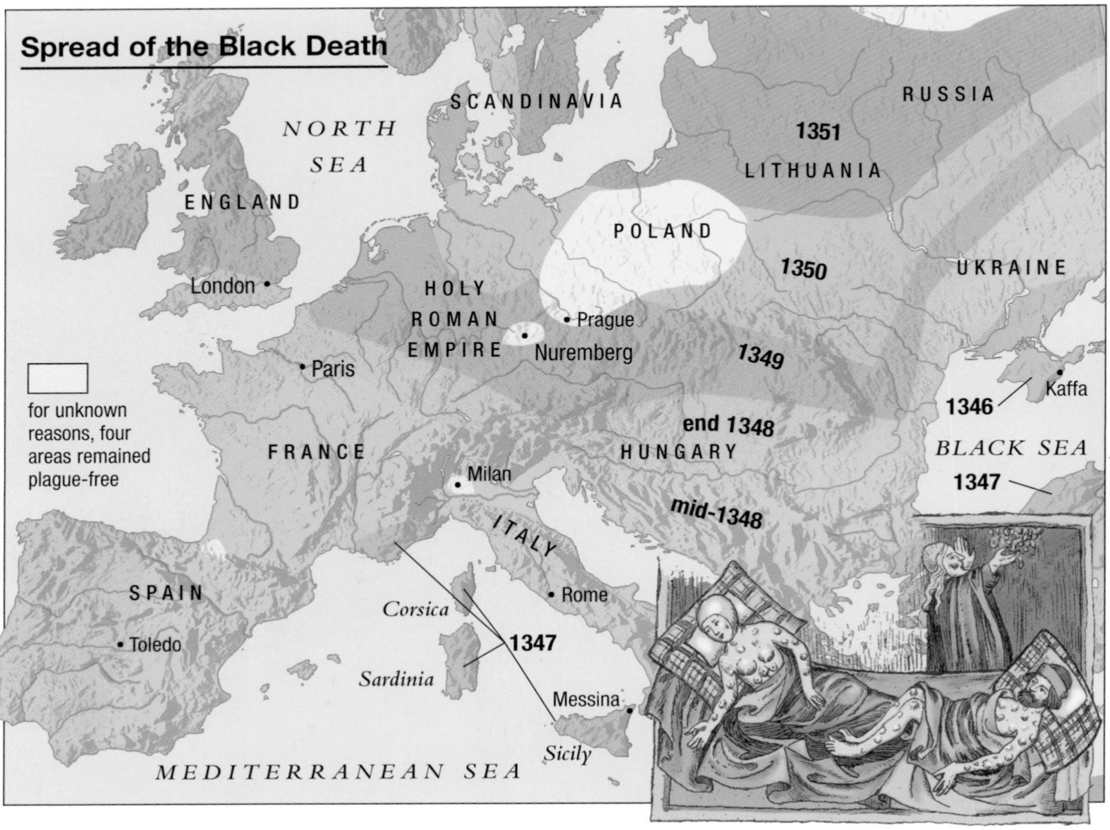

**Above:** Rats and their parasitic fleas spread the disease.

**Left:** Two sufferers of the bubonic plague, from the 15th-century Toggenberg Bible.

**Above right:** All across Europe the same scenes are repeated, as tens of thousands fall victim to the rat-borne plague. Soon, the burial grounds are full and civic authorities must dig mass graves to take the heavy loads of the tumbrel carts. Survivors grow used to the cry of "Bring out your dead!"

**Right:** A procession of Flagellants.

Reports tell of the seamen all dying within a week of their arrival. Days later, and most of the population of Messina fell ill. Within months, the disease had spread to Italy, and from there throughout the countries of Europe. The French doctor Simon de Covino has said that it seems as if one victim "could infect the whole world."

The Black Death is bubonic plague, a disease spread from rats to humans by parasitic fleas. In a society where hygiene is an unknown word, the disease spreads with ease. The initial symptoms are high temperatures, aching limbs, and lymph node swellings or 'buboes.' The plague attacks the lungs with effects similar to those of pneumonia, and the disease is invariably fatal. Other symptoms include internal bleeding, boils, and fever. The victim feels a profound depression, and death usually comes after three to five days.

## Empty towns and villages

Although some towns and villages escape the disease, the effects are dreadful. Even in lightly affected areas the mortality rate is 15–20 percent, and in the worst hit regions well over 50 percent have died—in all, about 20 million people throughout Europe.

In towns, the aftereffects are causing a complete collapse of the economy. As the dead become too numerous to be given Christian burial, their corpses lie in the streets, accelerating the spread of the disease. In the countryside, peasants drop dead in the fields and wayfarers at the roadside.

As usual in times of crisis, innocent scapegoats are held responsible for the calamity, especially the Jewish communities. It is said that in German towns, the Jews are being massacred, even though they have suffered from the Black Death as much as everyone else.

## The wrath of God

To ordinary people, it is obvious that either God has abandoned them or He has visited His anger on them for all their sins. One group in particular has decided to take on themselves the woes of the world and inflict self-punishment. They are called the Flagellants, and they wander from village to town, thrashing their almost naked bodies with scourges and whips until their flesh bleeds.

Many other extremist groups have also sprung up, but with the priesthood decimated, there is little the Church can do to prevent them spreading their strange beliefs among the weary survivors.

So severe is the population loss that the fields go untended, livestock is left to starve, and it seems as though it will take many years for the continent to recover from the Black Death.

# CHAPTER 4

# Life in a Medieval Town

## The Growth of Towns

Before the Black Death, most towns had been little more than marketplaces for the selling of local produce. But a series of social revolutions has changed all that.

The small village of Ludford as seen on pages 16–17 has changed beyond recognition. Much of the surrounding forest has vanished, a stone bridge has replaced the ford, and a large stone castle now stands in place of the old wooden motte and bailey.

Many houses of various sizes surround the castle and the chapel, which is now a bishop's cathedral. Due to the many wars of the earlier medieval period, the center of Ludford is protected by a defensive wall, although many houses and peasant huts huddle outside. How did this transformation take place?

### Wool brings a new prosperity

There are several reasons for Ludford's expansion. Some growth had occurred during the 12th and 13th centuries, but in part the Black Death had a hand. In its wake, many survivors living in the depopulated countryside migrated to the nearest urban centers for protection and to find work and food. The great landowners have taken advantage of the fall in rural population by enclosing great areas of arable fields to pasture for cattle and sheep grazing.

Wool is in huge demand all over Europe, and fortunes are to be made from its sale, especially to the Flemish cloth-makers of northern Belgium and France. In turn, this has pushed even more peasants off their lands to find a living in the towns and cities.

With more people coming to live in the town, like many others Ludford has had to expand its accommodation and services, which means more bureaucrats to administer civil matters. In turn, the administrators want servants, better houses, finer clothes, and more furniture and luxuries to show off their status, which means more craftsmen to make them. Artisans need bigger and better equipped workshops and apprentices to help them. They are the town's burghers, the start of a new middle class of citizens, owning property and ambitious to prosper further.

The cathedral, too, now requires numerous clerics to manage its affairs in the diocese and local parishes. These men must be well educated, so the cathedral has added a school and a university, which is welcomed by the town's burghers.

Another class of worker has sprung up. With its valuable wool trade, the river is now busy with barges transporting the woolen bales down river to the mouth, where a port has been built. Ludford is growing larger every day.

**1.** The abbey.

**2.** Parish churches.

**3.** The cathedral.

**4.** The market hall in the main square.

**5.** The Tabard, town inn.

**6.** The lord-knight's castle.

**7.** Grammar school.

**8.** Stone bridge and toll gate.

**9.** Fairground.

**10.** Water mill.

**11.** Fish pond.

1
2
5
4
3
6
7
2
10
9
8

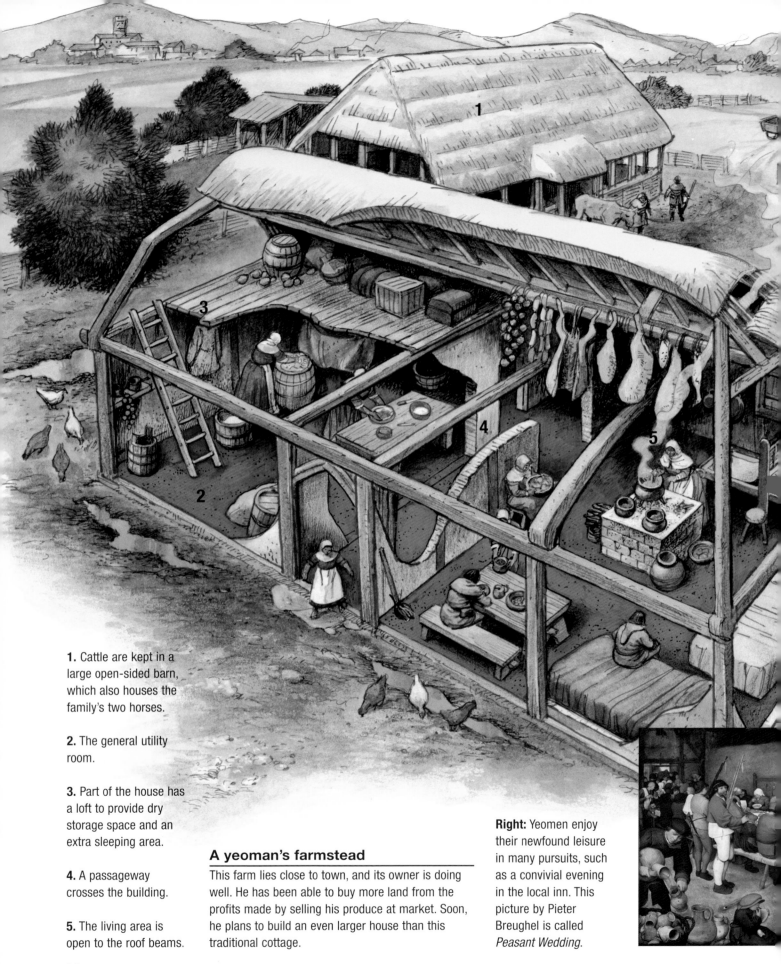

**1.** Cattle are kept in a large open-sided barn, which also houses the family's two horses.

**2.** The general utility room.

**3.** Part of the house has a loft to provide dry storage space and an extra sleeping area.

**4.** A passageway crosses the building.

**5.** The living area is open to the roof beams.

## A yeoman's farmstead

This farm lies close to town, and its owner is doing well. He has been able to buy more land from the profits made by selling his produce at market. Soon, he plans to build an even larger house than this traditional cottage.

**Right:** Yeomen enjoy their newfound leisure in many pursuits, such as a convivial evening in the local inn. This picture by Pieter Breughel is called *Peasant Wedding*.

# A New Middle Class—the Yeoman

In the later Middle Ages, the role of the peasant has altered. There are still serfs and *villeins* on the larger estates of nobles, but the Black Death has had a profoundly beneficial effect for many.

After the Black Death, the countryside has emptied out—a consequence of several famines and the ravages of the plague itself. It might be thought that this has caused hardship for the serfs shackled to the land. In fact, the opposite is the truth—the peasants have never been so well off.

## A labor market

Because so many perished in the plague, there is now a serious shortage of field labor. As a result, in the 1370s living standards have risen considerably as wages have gone up accordingly. No longer are the peasants of Europe prepared to endure the burdens they once suffered, they want freedom from their traditional feudal obligations.

With law and order broken down during the epidemic, many survivors were forced to leave the land on which their families had lived and toiled for generations in search of shelter and food in the small nearby towns.

This has given the post-plague peasant a sense of mobility never before experienced. He also feels that there are means of improving his situation by the example of the freer citizens of the town, who hire out their services. In fact, this period is one in which the workforce has the upper hand.

## Peasants become land owners

A second consequence of the Black Death is the plentiful land that can be obtained cheaply with the improved wages. For the first time, medieval peasants are becoming land-owners, or freeholders.

Naturally, this situation does not appeal to the feudal overlords, who—already short of *villeins*—are losing tenant farmers to the freedom of their own holdings. And the nobles are obliged to pay more in wages to keep the few *villeins* they do still have.

A freeholder of land is called a yeoman, a status well below that of the old landed gentry and nobles, but considerably above that of peasant. The "gentleman farmer" lets his land to tenant farmers rather than farm the land himself, but the yeoman is happy to work his fields and livestock himself. However, the successful yeoman can also afford to dip into the labor market and hire peasants to help him.

In this way, some yeomen, especially those with land close to a town and its market, have expanded by using their profits to purchase even more land. This gives a yeoman something the peasant never had, an opportunity for leisure time.

## Learning to live with freedom

While a yeoman is equally comfortable shovelling manure on his farm, he also uses his spare time to educate himself. He can afford to learn to write and read from books, or he can enjoy country sports such as shooting and hunting.

In the 14th century, some yeomen have earned a status as leaders in their district—constables, sheriffs, justices of the peace, even mayors. As a consequence, the yeoman has quickly developed into a respectable and honorable middle class of society.

### The fighting yeoman

Retainers of a fairly high rank in noble households are also called yeomen, and the name is often given to specific branches of the royal household, for instance Yeomen of the Guard.

The yeoman represents a status between the aristocratic knight and the lower-class man-at-arms and household servants. The famous English longbowmen are mostly yeomen, usually mounted for mobility but fighting on foot. In the countryside, yeomen are commonly organized into military units, who hire their services to the king when required. The yeoman foot soldiers of the Hundred Years War (1337–1453) being fought between England and France are the troops most personally in the service of the king.

# A New Middle Class—the Burgher

In German, the word "burg" means a fortified place. Since most medieval towns are protected by walled fortifications, those who live in them are called burghers. They are solid citizens of the merchant class, a dynamic force in medieval society.

It would be an error to think that town and country are separate entities; they rely heavily on each other. Without a surplus of food produced in the surrounding countryside, a town is unlikely to grow and prosper. The food markets of a small town also provide a place where merchants can ply their more specialist wares in sufficient quantity to bring down prices.

As a result, the peasants benefit from the cheaper costs of items such as cooking pots and clothing. And the shoppers, especially the yeomen who now have more income to spend, help to create a larger pool of craftsmen to supply their needs.

## Bustling streets

Established towns act as magnets for those peasants who migrated after the Black Death or who have been thrown off their land in favor of sheep-raising for the wool trade, and consequently their populations increase. Compared to the country, the town is a colorful, exciting place. All across Europe towns have developed almost independently of the nobility, and their inhabitants feel freer than the feudal peasant.

The town's merchant burghers are not forced to obey a distant lord, instead they follow the regulations of their elected mayor and other civic officers. They work to benefit themselves and their families, not a baron, and they pay their taxes to the king directly. And if it becomes necessary they raise the money to pay mercenaries to defend their town.

## The drive for education

The proud burgher is a stalwart supporter of good civic administration—a well-run and orderly town is good for business. He is also very visible in doing "good works" for the Church, and a regular giver of alms to support the poor and needy. In the wake of the Black Death, there are all too many who are still destitute.

**Below:** The Bavarian town of Augsburg is typical of the new, wealthy centers of trade and manufacture. Its citizens are freer to make their own laws than ever before. A new prosperity makes it possible to pay for extensive defensive walls to protect the inhabitants in times of unrest or war.

One aspect the burgher and the yeoman has in common is a yearning for education as a natural consequence of the greater time for leisure pursuits. Education is an important aspect in raising his children, especially the boys. This has led to a great demand for books written in the vernacular (local language) and not in traditional Latin, which few outside the Church any longer understand.

It has also sparked a spate of school buildings to provide a basic education for middle-class children. Unlike a noble, a burgher would never send his son away to be a page in a noble's household. He keeps his family together, and wants his sons to inherit the business and expand it to support as many sons as they might have.

A strictly formal education might lead a son to becoming a lawyer, possibly a clergyman, but for the burgher there is no shame in his son being apprenticed through one of the trade guilds (*see pages 68–69*).

## Status in color and quality

Along with the increased social status of the burgher comes a desire for better housing and quality of clothing. One of the wealthiest trades is that of cloth-making, for which the Flemish are renowned. But even more exotic, lighter weight fabrics have arrived from the Orient with soldiers returning from the Crusades.

The burgher's home may well be the place where he works, but it is also where he entertains other merchants, many of them business contacts from foreign countries. The growth in international trade created by the new middle class merchants requires a better means of payment than bartering, and so has driven the need for a greater use of coins (*see pages 82–83*). But above all, the burgher's home is a place of ease and comfort, as unlike the old serf's hut as chalk is from cheese.

Duke Philip of Burgundy greets a noble, who offers him a translation of the Koran in front of a monastic church and a town, with the larger city of Mussy-l'Eveque in the distance. The houses of the town-dwelling burghers (*bourgoisie* in French) now look much more comfortable than the drafty halls of previous years.

1
2
3
4
5
5
6

1. First floor shop, open to the street. The pivoted shutters to close it off at night are also used as trestle counters to display wares for sale.

2. Front door leading to passage.

3. Two-storied living hall, with central hearth.

4. Kitchen, pantry, and scullery area.

5. Upper floor bed chamber with simple furnishings.

6. Primitive toilet which is shared communally with neighbors.

7. Backyard, with chickens and a pig.

# A Burgher's House

A town house has many features in common with the rural manor house, although the extent and complexity depends on the owner's wealth.The medieval merchant's house combines several functions—home, workshop, office, and streetside store.

The design of most burghers' homes is determined largely by lack of space in the crowded streets. Town land is valuable, and the normal lot is long and narrow, running back from the street.

The usual house plan is rectangular, with the gable end facing onto the street. The frontage on the lower floor is divided between a shop and the main entrance to the house. Behind this is the living hall, often rising to two stories. Screens or tapestry hangings divide the hall to form a passageway from the entrance door to the pantries and kitchen.

A centrally placed hearth allows for a blazing fire in the winter months. Smoke escapes through a hole in the roof which is covered by a louvre. Several of the richer burghers are now building brick chimneys against an outer wall to provide larger and safer fires, and the chimney also draws out the smoke more efficiently.

On the upper floor there is room for one or more bed chambers above the passage and shop, reached by narrow stairs to a balcony overlooking the hall. Extra space is gained by extending the floor out over the street.

## The ever-present risk of fire

The kitchen and scullery is sometimes a detached structure at the rear, separated from the main house by a courtyard, or it might sit beneath an overhang of the main building. Further back is the counting house. Depending on space, a workshop and warehouses might be attached to the house, or separated by the yard.

The better off might afford to build at least the lower floor's walls of stone or brick, but most burghers' houses are timber-framed with wattle walls. This means that they are a fire risk, and the closeness of adjacent buildings, with their overhanging upper floors, greatly adds to the risk of fire spreading.

## Privies and privacy

Despite its obvious comforts compared to a peasant's hut, there is very little privacy, since everyone congregates in the hall to keep warm, enjoy recreation, eat, and even to sleep. If there is room for a second bed chamber on the upper floor, it is likely that all the children will have to sleep together in it. The one or two servants bunk down in the scullery, while any apprentices make their beds in the master's workshop.

There are no proper sanitation facilities. Water is brought daily by carriers from the river or town well. The most that the family might hope for is a very occasional tub of heated water for a bath, taken in the hall behind a temporary screen. However, some personal hygiene can be obtained at one of the town's "stews," or public baths.

Privies or garderobes are made in the thickness of the walls of larger houses, or as projecting jetties in lesser ones. The privy discharges through pipes and gutters into a cesspit at the rear of the house. These are regularly cleaned out in the "night cartage of filth" by "men of the night soil" trade. At night, chamber pots are commonly used, their noxious contents usually thrown out of the window into the street below.

## Home comforts

Even in the wealthier homes, there is little furniture. Typical furnishings might include a table covered with a linen cloth, benches or forms, a chair, stools, chests and small cupboards and shelves for cups, jugs, pewter, knives and spoons, bowls and plates.

The house is a drafty place, for the windows generally have no glass in them and only have shutters. Some merchants can afford to fill the spaces between the window "mullions" with thin-shaved horn, which cuts down the drafts and still allows a little daylight through. Only the very rich can afford the huge cost of glass.

# A Flowering of Styles

Town dwellers have access to an increasing range of cloth and luxury fabrics for both men and women.

Since the Crusades, the skills of oriental weavers and cloth-makers have been imported to Europe with the returning crusader knights. From Damascus comes the intricately patterned damask, from Mosul the diaphanous muslin, from Gaza gauze, and from Egypt bales of cotton.

These fabrics have transformed late medieval costume from the drabness of earlier years. The tired old grays and russet-browns are out. Latest fashions call for strikingly colored doublets and hose, sweeping cloaks trimmed with ermin or sable collars, and softly fashioned leather shoes.

## Age of the dandy

Rural dress remains much as it had in the earlier Middle Ages, coarse sack cloth over woolen undergarments, but in the towns "flamboyance" is the key word. Never before has fashion reached such extravagant heights.

Exotic dyes from the Orient permit lavish use of color, with vivid stripes and large harlequin checks very popular for men. For the younger man, extremely tight-fitting hose (stockings) in bright reds, greens, blues and softer hues are fashionable.

Over the upper body, a tunic called a doublet is worn that flares out from the waist into a short "skirt." The doublet might also be body-fitting or loose and flowing, and padded shoulders (*mahoîtres*) give the young blade a dashing, powerful appearance. Garments are often decorated by "dagging"—purposely made slashes in ornamental zigzags, often revealing a strongly contrasting color underneath.

## Feet a victim of fashion

A wide range of shoes is available, but the typical dandy likes ones with extremely long pointed toes. Some have such extended points that the tips have to be chained up and fastened at the knee for the owner to walk safely.

Headwear matches the men's clothing in its color, and the fashion-conscious man is rarely seen bare headed. A popular style of hat is the high Burgundian cap, but wider and flatter broad-brimmed soft caps are common. These are often draped with a liripipe, a soft scarf that is finished by being draped over the left shoulder.

**Top:** Fashionable envoys with their pointed shoes, padded shoulders and body-hugging doublets and hose greet the French king.

**Center:** A lawcourt official in his grand cape carries an additional soft cap and cape over his shoulder.

Above: Ladies wearing hennin hats of butterfly wings attend a baby's baptism.

**Above:** The fashion for ever more pointed men's shoes becomes ridiculous.

**Opposite:** Isabella of Bourbon, wife of Charles the Bold Duke of Burgundy, poses in a tall conical hennin.

## Hats like sailing ships

Women are clothed in a fanciful array of garments. Low-cut dresses with long sleeves covering the hands are usually worn with voluminous trains (a serving girl is an essential accessory to keep the train from dragging in the muddy street). Dresses usually have a high, narrow waistline, secured by a wide belt.

The hat of choice is called a *hennin*. This is a tall conical headdress adorned with starched linen wings like a butterfly, or with a long, flowing veil draped from the point of the cone and dropped over an arm. Reticulated (wire mesh) hats are also popular with women, and some of these reach extraordinary proportions of complexity in shape, wide side horns being in fashion.

Nobles tend to follow the new burgher fashions, sometimes to extremes. For instance, the churchmen have issued edicts forbidding young noblemen from wearing ultra-short tunics that reveal more tightly-hosed leg than they consider proper.

### The sumptuary laws

The Church and the nobles disapprove of the extravagance of modern fashions among commoners in their trimmed furs and glittering jewelry. In showing off their finery, the lower classes are thought to be threatening the established feudal order. So many European countries have passed "sumptuary" laws to regulate what a person may wear, so as not to compete with the vivid styles of the aristocracy. Where these laws are in force, merchants are only allowed to wear long dark robes and a *capuchon*, the hat favored by commoners rich and poor. This hood has a short cape extending over the shoulders, but many merchants, like these below greedily counting their money, push the sumptuary laws to the limit by twisting the cape up on their heads like a turban.

# Merchants Gang Up

A medieval guild (also spelled "gild") is an association formed for mutual aid and protection, and to further the professional interests of its members. Medieval guilds are of two types, the merchant and craft guilds.

The first merchant guilds were formed early in the Middle Ages for mutual protection of their horses, wagons, and goods when traveling. In the late 14th century, their originally modest aims have changed enormously. The merchant guilds have the recognition of the town's government, which is hardly surprising since the wealthiest and most influential citizens are councilors.

Indeed, it is often one or other of the most powerful of the guilds that dictates policy to the town council. It is not uncommon to find that the council members are entirely drawn from among the ranks of the guildsmen.

The merchants' guilds are intimately involved in regulating and protecting their members' interests, both in long-distance trade and local town business. Each distinct guild in a town is in constant touch with its fellow guilds in other towns and cities, and even their foreign counterparts.

Guilds control the distribution and sale of food, cloth, and other staple goods, which gives them a powerful monopoly, and together they form a network of communication that exceeds that of many European rulers' governments. The most powerful of the European guilds is the Hanseatic League (*see page 89*), virtually an empire of its own.

## Craft guilds

These were formed later than the merchant guilds, and at first were considered to be less important. Craft guilds are associations of all the artisans and craftsmen in a particular branch of industry or commerce. For example, there are guilds of stonemasons, architects, weavers, dyers, embroiderers, bookbinders, painters, metalworkers, bakers, and leatherworkers.

The craft guilds are now as influential as the merchant guilds, and demand a share of the civic leadership. As craftsmen travel a great deal less than merchants, they have the advantage of being nearby to make sure the town is run how they like it.

In this way, the guilds can control many aspects of town life, such as how many masters may operate within a particular skill. As a group, the guildsmen regulate competition among themselves, set minimum quality standards, prevent price-cutting, and ensure their trade monopoly within the town by forbidding outside workers from setting up business.

The skilled craftsmen in a town usually consist of a number of family workshops in the same neighborhood, with the masters related to each other, often sharing apprentices between them. Members of the craft guilds are divided into three skill and status levels—master, journeyman, and apprentice.

Members of a guild stand proudly before the steps and grand entranceway to their guildhall. In some cases, the guildhall of the largest guilds, such as the haberdashers, who make clothing accessories, or mercers (cloth merchants), even acts as the town hall, from which the town council hands down local bylaws.

**Left:** A master apothecary (pharmacist) proudly shows off what his seated apprentice has already learned.

**Right:** Craftsmen, unlike merchants, are tied to their town. The one exception is the mason. Good masons are in demand all over Europe to work on castles, churches, and cathedrals. They work under a lean-to shelter called a lodge. Because they are free to travel, they are referred to as "free masons."

## A long route to the top

The master—an experienced and expert craftsman—owns his own home, workshop (often the same place), and the tools of his trade. Most importantly, the master is a member of his trade's guild and is therefore authorized to take on apprentices for training and to help him in his work.

The apprentices he employs are usually adolescent boys (girls are not allowed to be apprenticed). Apprentices are provided with food, clothing, shelter, and an education by the master, in return for working without pay for a fixed term of service of about five to nine years. At the end of his apprenticeship, the young man becomes a journeyman, and may work for his or another master and be paid modest wages for his labor.

Many craftsmen remain at this level for the rest of their working lives. To take the next step up, the journeyman must provide his guild with proof of his technical and artistic skills by making a "masterpiece."

If he is approved, the guild declares him a master and full guild member. He can then set up his own workshop, and hire and train apprentices. However, even the most skilled artisan might have to wait for ages to become a master. Because the guild regulates how many masters may operate at any one time, promotion is often a matter of stepping into a dead man's shoes.

**Above:** Among good works provided by burghers are foundling (orphans') hospitals and infirmaries for the poor, as well as their own guild members.

## The guilds' welfare state

Both the merchant and craft guilds perform similar additional services for their members. They provide funeral expenses for poorer members and aid to widows and orphans, offer dowries for poorer families' daughters, cover members' health insurance, and make provision for care of the sick.

As worthy members of the holy congregation, the guilds build chapels, donate windows to local churches or cathedrals, and often help fund the expensive enlargement of existing churches. They also act as guardians of the morals of their members and other citizens.

Perhaps the guilds' biggest contribution to medieval society is to found and finance "grammar" schools for the education of their members' sons.

Children of the middle class can now receive a basic education from a clergyman at one of the new grammar schools.

# The Rise of Education and Universities

For hundreds of years, the only schools have been under the Church's control, but the rise of the burgher middle class has created a demand for more widespread education.

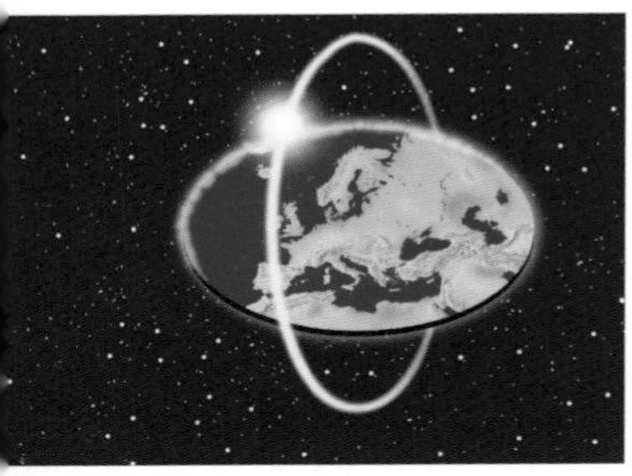

It is well known that the sun revolves around the earth, which is a flat disk (above), but new philosophers argue that the earth revolves about the sun, which makes them heretics to the Roman Catholic Church.

Monasteries remain the oldest centers of learning in Europe, but these are places of piety rather than schools of theology and philosophical debate. Such as it exists, education in a monastery is primarily for the monks and not children.

Cathedral schools in the larger cities, which grew up in the 12th and 13th centuries, have a role similar to that of the monastic schools. They typically have fewer than a hundred students and function as seminaries to train future priests.

Since many pupils will be more administrators than pastors, an emphasis is placed on teaching the "liberal" arts, particularly philosophy and literary study. Some cathedral schools have grown beyond the constraints of purely religious instruction and developed specialization in particular fields. For example, in France, Orléans is noted for literary study and Paris for philosophy and theology, while Bologna in Italy is famous for the study of Roman law (*see pages 74–75*) on which European justice is based. These institutions have become universities.

## Learning to read and write

In the early Middle Ages, education for children was scarce, restricted to the religious schooling of sons of the noble elite. But with the growth of towns and the rise of the merchant middle class, new schools for children are springing up.

These "grammar" schools are usually run by clerics, but they are teaching the children of many townspeople to read, write, and count, as well as giving religious instruction. The son of a merchant who does well here will go on to further his education at one of the new universities.

## Further education

A university is distinguished from any other type of school by its official charter (granted by a royal or ecclesiastical authority), called a set of statutes. This grants the university the right to govern itself.

Many universities have grown out of the cathedral schools, such as that at Paris, which developed after 1150 and received its statutes in 1215. The Sorbonne became associated with the university in 1257. The term *universitas* refers to the "entirety" (*universality*) of scholars, both faculty and students.

A faculty for philosophy

Universities have four "faculties"—arts, law, medicine, and theology. The arts faculty is a foundation course to one of the "higher" faculties. Study of ancient philosophy is a major part of the arts, but the Church is unhappy with the teachings of many ancient thinkers, such as Aristotle (384–322 BC), who places man above the need for any god, and Aristarchus (270 BC). Both these Greek thinkers were "heliocentrists," men who insist that the earth revolves about the sun. This is in contradiction to the Church's "geocentric" view, that the sun revolves about the earth, which is believed to be at the center of the solar system.

## The spread of universities from the 12th to the 15th centuries

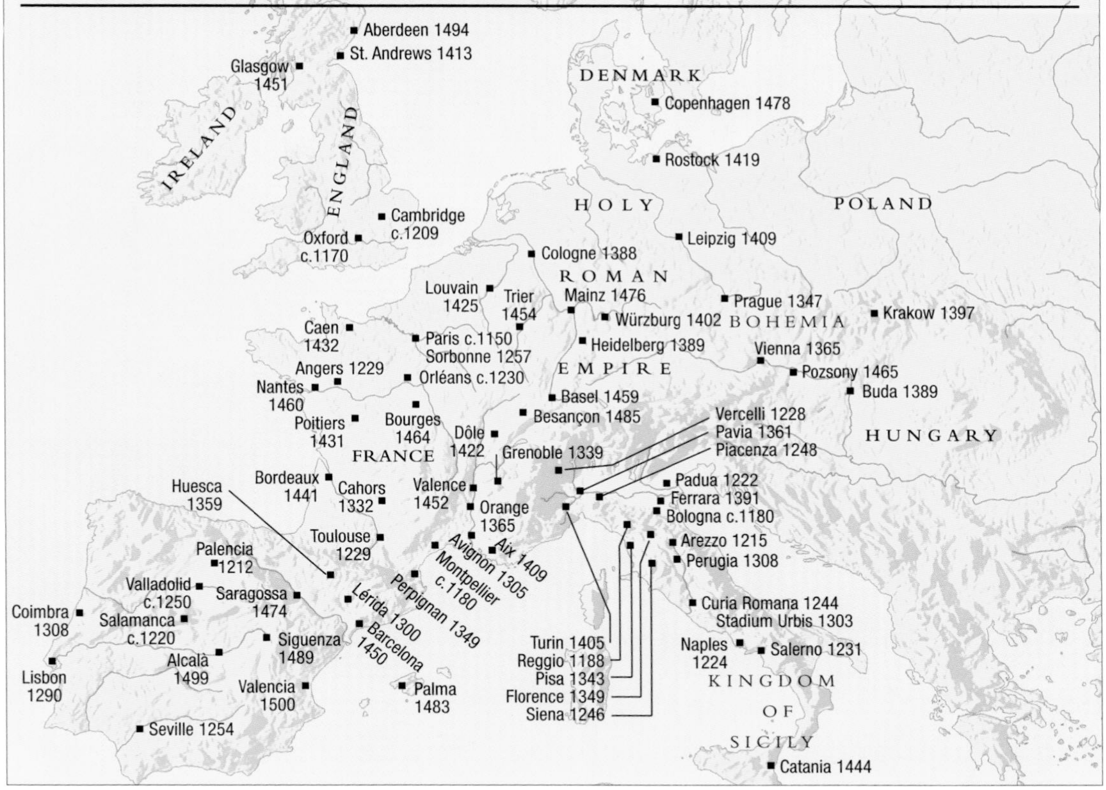


## Stamping on the new learning

By their very nature, universities bring together masters and students from all over Europe and put them in close proximity. This has resulted in a boom in academic study, including philosophy, with its seductive new and revolutionary ideas. At the same time, such large bodies of energetic, free-thinking young men, living in a self-governing body, get rowdy at the drop of a hat.

Massive drinking bouts lead to heated debates and often fists and even blades. This may be enormous fun for the students, but when their fights spill over into the town streets, it is miserable for the citizens. Such is the state of tension between "gown and town" in England's famous Oxford University that open warfare often exists between the townspeople and the student body.

While student horseplay is a natural way for boisterous youths to let off steam, when the pope bans the teaching of works by the likes of Aristotle, violence erupts as the entire faculty riots. In this way, Church leaders view the modern universities with deep suspicion, and several have even been shut down by Church edict amid bitter street brawling.

**Right:** Troubadors, or minstrels wander all over Europe. The storytellers of the Middle Ages, their romantic poems are the content for many new books.

**Left:** A 19th-century engraving depicts the death of Roland, a brave French knight who fought in the Battle of Ronçesvalle against the Moors. The *Song of Roland* is one of the most popular themes.

**Below:** A page from Chaucer's highly popular pilgrim stories, *Canterbury Tales*.

# Books and the New Literature

Greater disposable income, increased time for leisure, and a desire for education means that the new middle classes want to read—not only traditional Church texts, but also non-religious literature.

In the early Middle Ages, hardly anyone except churchmen could read, and literature was almost exclusively of a Christian nature. The situation was made worse because the printed words were all in Latin, the language of the Church and of law but not of the common people.

Throughout Europe, vernacular—the local non-Latin language such as German, French, or Italian—was only spoken, rarely written down. England is an exception, since written English has been in use for legal documents and some poetry since the 9th century.

## Woodblock printing

As a consequence of the newfound prosperity and better education, people are demanding the written word in their own languages, and the production of books in the vernacular is growing accordingly. The Bible, once the preserve of educated churchmen, is the most wanted book, but a demand for romantic poetry and entertaining prose is on the increase.

At one time, books were produced by monks in their *scriptoria*, and the time consuming job of copying texts by hand meant few books were ever produced. Woodblock printing changed that. The process of carving large blocks of wood with letters and illustrations is still labor-intensive and slow, but once finished, hundreds of imprints can be taken from a single block.

A sheet of paper is laid over the inked woodblock and an impression taken by rubbing over the paper with a roller. Now an even better system is revolutionizing book printing (*see "Gutenberg's press"*).

## Telling a good story

Books popular among the burghers are often ones with themes of derring-do and romance, the exploits of knights of old and damsels in distress. The romantic verses of 9th century Frankish historian Einhardt describing the life of Charlemagne the Great and Geoffrey of Monmouth's history rewritten as the romantic *Sir Gawain and the Green Knight* are both popular titles from an earlier age.

So too are the French *Song of Roland* and the Spanish *El Cid*, although more modern

fictions such as the mythological *The Nibelungenlied*, Wolfram von Eschenbach's *Parsival*, and *Narratives* by the French writer Chrétien de Troyes are showing better sales.

## A series of tall tales

Without doubt, the author whose work is most on everyone's lips these days is the Englishman Geoffrey Chaucer (c.1345–1400), with his *Canterbury Tales*.

Chaucer's life itself reads like a work of romance. Born into a wealthy middle class London family, he has traveled widely in Europe, picking up French and Italian influences. He has been an international diplomat, clerk of the king's works, and his patron is John of Gaunt, regent of England.

The *Canterbury Tales* recounts the several stories told by a group of pilgrims to entertain themselves as they make their way to visit St. Becket's shrine at Canterbury Cathedral. Witty, exciting, and often shockingly vulgar, the different tales are a showcase of the modern vernacular.

They also arouse the disapproval of the Church. But the genie is out of the bottle—the more people read about life, begin to understand the written words of the Bible, come across the writings of ancient Roman and Greek philosophers, the more they begin to question the Roman Catholic Church's interpretation of Christian belief.

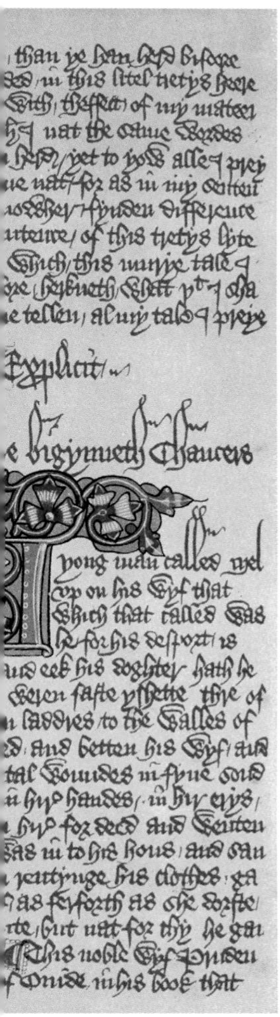
Explicit
e biginneth Chaucers

## Gutenberg's press

Johannes Gutenberg (c.1396–1468), a German goldsmith, is best known for the innovative printing machine that uses movable type. Instead of text cut into wood blocks as whole pages, in the Gutenberg system the text is split up into individual components—lower and upper case letters and punctuation marks.

Each character is cut into the end face of a steel punch, resulting in a precise shape in reverse. Then the punch is hammered on a rectangular block made of softer metal, such as copper, to form a letter shape raised above the block level.

The individual component blocks are then arranged on a wooden form to make words. The form has raised rails of lead to keep the lines of text straight and evenly spaced vertically.

When a page is fully composed, the form, with all its letters locked in place, is placed on the press, inked, and impressed onto a sheet of prepared paper. Because the metal letters are harder wearing than the old woodblocks, a great many more pages can be printed than previously. On September 30, 1452, Johannes Gutenberg's Bible was published, becoming the first book to be published in volume.

# A Hodge-Podge of Laws

Medieval law is in flux, with four overlapping and sometimes conflicting systems of trial and justice. Whichever law applies, for the common man the outcome is invariably harsh.

**Above:** A big trial finds a nobleman guilty of treason.

Without law and order, a society finds it hard to progress, but most laws seem to be for the benefit of the clergy and the nobility. Those in authority fear the poor, simply because there are so many more poor than rich, and any revolt is potentially damaging. As a result, punishment is designed to deter wrongdoers and act as a frightening example to others to make them behave properly.

## Old laws still linger

Although the oldest form of medieval European law is no longer recognized, its effects can still be felt in unruly cities and in rural regions. It is based on the customs and traditions of the German barbarians who entered the Roman Empire toward its end. It follows the principle of "an eye for an eye," and depends on retribution for justice.

If the member of one clan should harm the member of another, in person or in property, the aggrieved person's relatives seek retribution through a vendetta.

The obvious drawback is that if the defending clan thinks the accusing clan is overreaching themselves, they are likely to seek their own retribution. Games of tit for tat like this can go on for years, long after the original complaint has been forgotten.

## The Barbarian Codes

The answer to the chaos caused by the laws governing vendettas was to reduce the traditions to a written form, the so-called Barbarian Codes. Under this system, disputants looked to their tribal chieftains to act as arbitrators. However, any decision

**Above and below:** Many accused are tempted to plead guilty rather than face trial by combat or being tossed bound into a pond.

**Far right:** A lecturer in the law sits at his lectern at the University of Bologna.

required establishing the facts of a case, which led to several means being developed that still remain.

The first, and apparently the most reasonable, is called "compurgation." This means that a person accused of a crime is required to swear an oath that he is innocent. He might be required to persuade a number of the leading members of his clan or family to swear the same oath along with him. If it turns out that the defendant is lying, he and all of his conspirators are liable to suffer the same punishment.

The second method is trial by ordeal, in which the accused is forced to undergo one of several tests to prove his innocence. In the trial of cold water the defendant is bound and thrown into a pond that has been blessed by a priest. Since the holy water will reject a liar, the guilty will float and the innocent sink.

Trial by fire requires the accused to walk three paces while holding a red hot iron bar. His hand is then bandaged and left for three days. After this time, a healing wound proves innocence while one that is not improving indicates guilt.

The third method—trial by combat—relies on the certainty that God will not allow the guilty to prosper. The plaintiff and defendant enter the field of combat, and fight until one is the clear victor or one lies dead. In many cases, especially among the nobility, neither party fights but chooses a champion to do battle in his place. Each combatant swears by the right of the cause of the person they represent and, in the ensuing combat, God will strengthen the arm of the innocent.

## Roman law

At the University of Bologna in Italy, teachers recently discovered the 6th-century Emperor Justinian's *Codex*. This had gathered all Roman law from the earliest days and rationalized any contradictions so that all would know what was expected of them. Its sophistication and emphasis on the supremacy of state authority recommends it to monarchs, although it often leads to conflict with the Church.

## Canon law

The Church controls matters that involve oaths, the sacraments, testaments, marriage and divorce, and even many business contracts. It also handles all matters of heresy and cases involving clergymen.

The Church enforces its edicts through what is called canon law, which is the body of laws and regulations made by or adopted by ecclesiastical authority, for the government of Christians everywhere. Those convicted under canon law may face excommunication or being burnt alive.

## Common law

The differing needs of monarchy, Church, commoners, and particularly the emerging middle class is leading toward a reduction of local laws and customs to a set of general principles. This is called common law.

But however sensible the attempts to make a universal set of laws may be, the result of a conviction for the guilty usually means a horrible punishment, one designed to fit the crime.

# Punishment Fits the Crime

For the accused who survive trial by ordeal or combat, or anyone convicted by a court under "compurgation," the future is sure to be full of pain, humiliation, and likely very short.

There is no concept of rehabilitation for convicts, and very few prisons exist because they cost money to build and manage. It is far cheaper to mutilate criminals and then let them go, or execute them. In the Middle Ages, the idea of punishment is to inflict pain as a means of society's revenge for a crime, and even the smallest offenses have serious punishments.

Thieves have their hands cut off. Women convicted of murder are strangled until almost dead and then burnt. Anyone caught stealing is likely to have their ears cut off. Hanging by the neck until dead is the punishment for armed robbery.

## Making an example for others

For high treason, the convict can look forward to the gruesome punishment of being hanged, drawn, and quartered. After being paraded through the streets and reviled by the towns' folk, the convict is strung up by the neck but taken down before he dies. Laid out on the ground, the executioner slices his belly open and "draws" out his entrails. Then, barely alive, he is cut into four "quarters" by the executioner.

Execution by beheading with sword or ax is reserved for members of the aristocracy, the severed head usually displayed on a pike stuck on the town wall or a bridge parapet.

Most towns have a gibbet just outside the walls. After their execution, the bodies of convicts are suspended on the gibbet from hooks and their bodies left to rot over the weeks as a warning to others.

However, the grisly example does not always have the desired effect. In 1202, the English city of Lincoln posted 114 murders, 89 violent robberies, and 65 people wounded in fights, yet only two men were executed. It seems that many in Lincoln get away with their crimes.

## A public ridicule

Minor first offenses—for instance, drunkenness in public, failing to pay rent, or shouting abuse at a civic dignitary—results in a spell in the stocks. Although painful enough through discomfort, it is the humiliation of being held in public that is the punishment, as people throw rotten eggs and vegetables at the victim.

Scolds—wives who nag their husbands—are sentenced to the ducking stool or to spend a period of time strapped into a "scold's bridle." Both punishments are physically distressing, but also a public humiliation.

Women charged with witchcraft are dealt with in the same way as heretics—those who publicly oppose the teachings of the Church. Their fate is to be tied to a stake atop a pile of wooden tinder and then burned to death while the public watches.

The array of punishments in the Middle Ages is great, and often the suffering of the victims is a source of amusement to the spectators.

**Left:** The pillory is a humiliating experience for anyone convicted of a minor crime. A similar device is called the stocks, in which only the ankles are imprisoned.

**Below left:** For the habitual nagger, the scold's bridle is a punishment of great discomfort.

**Below right:** Pressing is a form of torture that invariably leads to the victim's death.

## Horrors of the torturer

Torture is widely used, both as a means of forcing a confession and as a punishment. Few victims of the torturer's art survive for long, even if they are freed. The catalog of devices is long.

Wooden wedges forced underneath the toenails, clamps to force the jaws apart and scissors to slice the tongue, a copper boot placed around the victim's foot filled to the brim with molten lead. Thumbscrews, footpresses, and a chair of spikes are just a few more of the imaginative tools of the trade.

One of the commonest forms of torture is called pressing. The victim is made to lie on the floor, face up, and a large board is placed on his chest. Onto this, the torturer places heavy rocks, increasing the number as time goes by. Gradually, the weight crushes the victim, usually to death.

## There but for the grace of God

Whatever punishment is handed out, the common element is the public nature of the event. Whenever a hanging or burning is announced, the townspeople flock to the site, ready to enjoy one of the great entertainments of their day. It may seem heartless to take pleasure from the cruel punishment of others, but for many the joy is a simple one—it is not them to die.

# The Town Inn

The lowly village tavern, little more than a shack, is transformed in a large town into a magnificent center of middle class society—a place of companionship, gossip, and relaxation.

Ludford's main inn, the Tabard, is more than a drinking shop. It serves as a center of communication in many senses. Arranged around three sides of a large courtyard, the inn boasts stables with ostlers to look after travelers' horses, a large hall for customers, a well-equipped kitchen, and several guestrooms on the upper floor.

The inn also acts as a sort of post office, as people passing through leave verbal or written messages for other travelers or for townspeople, which the innkeeper will pass on when they appear.

For the local merchants, craftsmen, and yeomen, the Tabard is a meeting house where news and gossip is exchanged in a less formal atmosphere than the guildhalls. Here, gentlemen can relax over a pint of ale or a glass of wine, or perhaps a tasty meat stew, and debate town politics, the antics of the royal court, complain about poor town council decisions, and generally put the world to rights.

## Slight slumber comforts

Although the upper floor only has six bedrooms, on a busy night as many as 20 or more guests might be accommodated, piling them in four to a room to squabble over the cramped beds and their straw mattresses.

Sleep is difficult because of the constant roar of the inn's customers below, who are generally only thrown out when the innkeeper has had enough. Below in the yard, the clatter of hooves disturbs the night as latecomers arrive or early risers canter off to continue their journey.

However, a singular and welcome comfort is that for a small price, an overnight guest can arrange for a tub of hot water to be brought so that he might take a bath.

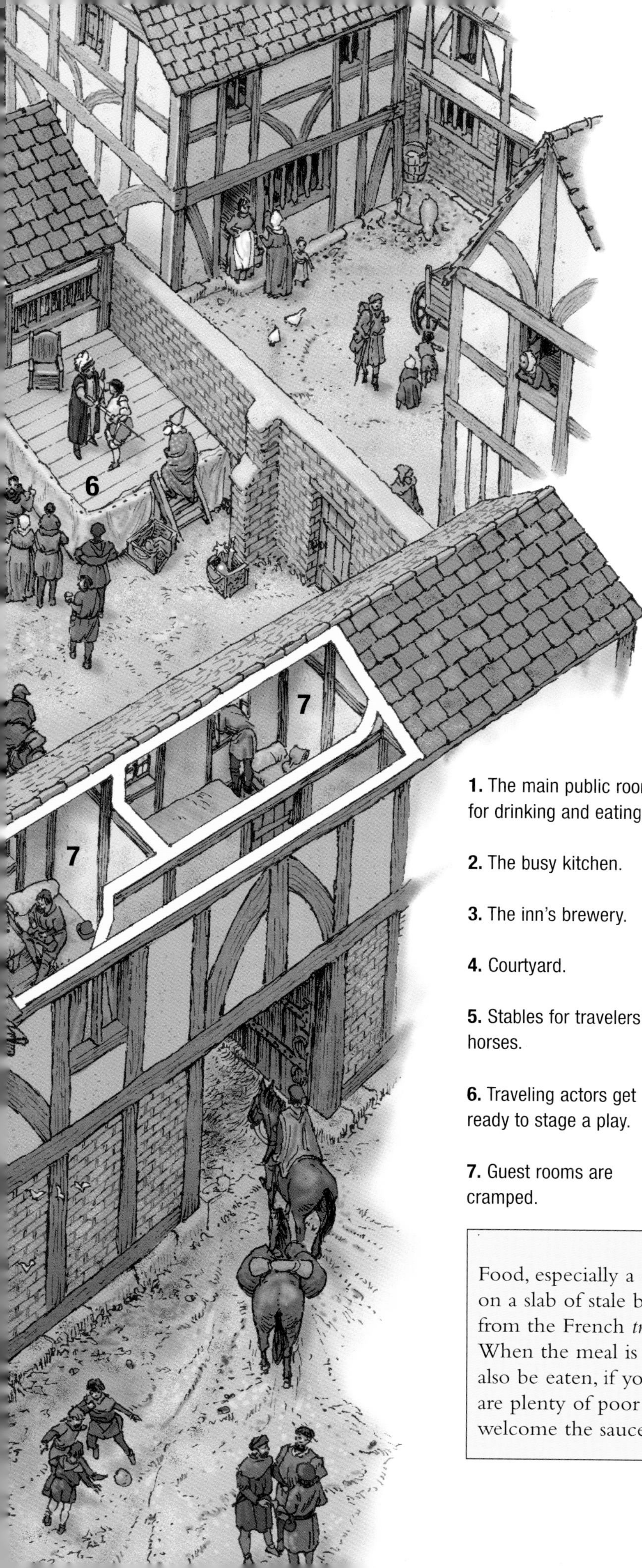


**1.** The main public room for drinking and eating.

**2.** The busy kitchen.

**3.** The inn's brewery.

**4.** Courtyard.

**5.** Stables for travelers' horses.

**6.** Traveling actors get ready to stage a play.

**7.** Guest rooms are cramped.

## Taking to the boards

Every so often, the inn's courtyard becomes home to a troupe of traveling actors, who set up a shaky stage of wooden boards at one end and charge an entry fee for the playgoers. Since the innkeeper takes a hefty cut of the "gate" and benefits from the increased patronage the play brings in and their demands for liquid refreshment, acting companies are always welcomed.

## The demon drink

Drinking, however, is the main activity at the Tabard. The inn has its own ale brewery out at the back, beyond the kitchen, but such is the quantity quaffed every day, that most of the ale is bought in.

Like every town, Ludford has brewers all up and down most streets. Many of these are women—brewing is one of the female population's largest trades. Ale is as necessary to life as bread, but where flour-grinding and bread-baking are strictly guarded monopolies, brewing is freely permitted everywhere.

Drinking bouts often end in unfortunate accidents as a result of intoxication. So we learn that one gentleman coming home at about midnight "drunk and disgustingly over-fed," fell and struck his head fatally on a stone "breaking the whole of his head." One man fell into a well in the marketplace and was "drownded," like another who, while relieving himself in a pond, fell in.

Men are not the only victims of their overindulgence, proved by the sad story of the mother whose child slipped from her drunken hands into a pan of scalding hot milk on the hearth.

On the other hand, an unknown monk has this to say on the question of drink: "He who drinks ale sleeps well. He who sleeps well cannot sin. He who does not sin goes to Heaven. Amen."

Food, especially a common stew, is served on a slab of stale bread called a trencher, from the French *trencher*, meaning "to cut." When the meal is finished, the trencher can also be eaten, if you are desperate, but there are plenty of poor people outside who will welcome the sauce-soaked chunk of bread.

# All the Entertainment of the Fair

In a life that consists mostly of toil, the annual event of the trade fair is a welcome break, a chance to enjoy rare free time with family and neighbors and generally make merry.

Throughout the Middle Ages, monarchs have encouraged trade fairs, both to foster trade and to profit from the tolls levied on the goods the merchants bring in for sale. The Ludford annual fair takes place just outside the town walls on a meadow specially reserved for it and lasts for several days in the early summer.

Within hours of their arrival, the merchants have set up a veritable town of tents and "streets," and each day the townsfolk stream out to partake of the fun. The commerce of the fair takes place amid a carnival atmosphere. Stilt-walkers tower over the crowds, jugglers and acrobats show off their skills, while musicians entertain the crowd by playing their lutes and beating tabor drums. For the ordinary people, this folk music is an exciting change from the plain religious chant of the church and cathedral.

## Bear-baiting and "monsters"

There are many sideshows for which people pay a modest entry fee. Spectacles involving animals are the most popular, such as dog- and cockfights. But the largest ring is the bear-baiting "pit," a circular structure of wood with seating inside around the ring.

The bear is chained to a strong stake at the center and a pack of dogs is released into the pit. Dogs go flying from the bear's powerful swipes, but some manage to inflict savage bites. Inevitably the bear wins out, which is as well for the spectacle's owner—dogs are cheap, bears are not.

Other stalls offer the amusement of viewing "monsters," unfortunate men and women with disfigurements, strongmen performing amazing physical stunts, and the chance for young men to show off their skills with the stave, or staff.

## Keep your hand on your purse

The fair is rigidly controlled by patrols of mounted guards, which is just as well, because the crowds attract every kind of petty thief, from "cutpurses" to "cony-catchers." Cutpurses sometimes work alone, using a sharp knife to sever the thongs holding an unwary man's money purse from his belt.

Sometimes they work in pairs, with one performing simple tricks with a dried pea and three thimbles to distract the victim while the other steals the purse. Cony-catchers are clever deceivers, conmen who cheat gullible gentlemen and ladies of their money with false tales.

A brightly painted tent houses a special fair court, known as *peid-poudre* (literally "dusty feet"), where disputes can be settled while those involved are still "dusty-footed."

## Passion and mummery

The annual fair is an opportunity to enjoy several acting entertainments, which are broadly divided into two types—secular and religious. The actors, often disguised by masks or heavy face paint, act out plays based on the themes of dual personality and resurrection. These allegories, which have a pagan feel, generally involve a battle representing good against evil. They usually feature a doctor who has a magic potion which is able to bring a slain character back to life. Some of the actors wear bells attached to their legs and perform complex movements called morris dancing.

# Coinage and Banking

Until the later Middle Ages, coins were rare, but the growth of towns and mercantile commerce has caused many more to be minted and put into circulation.

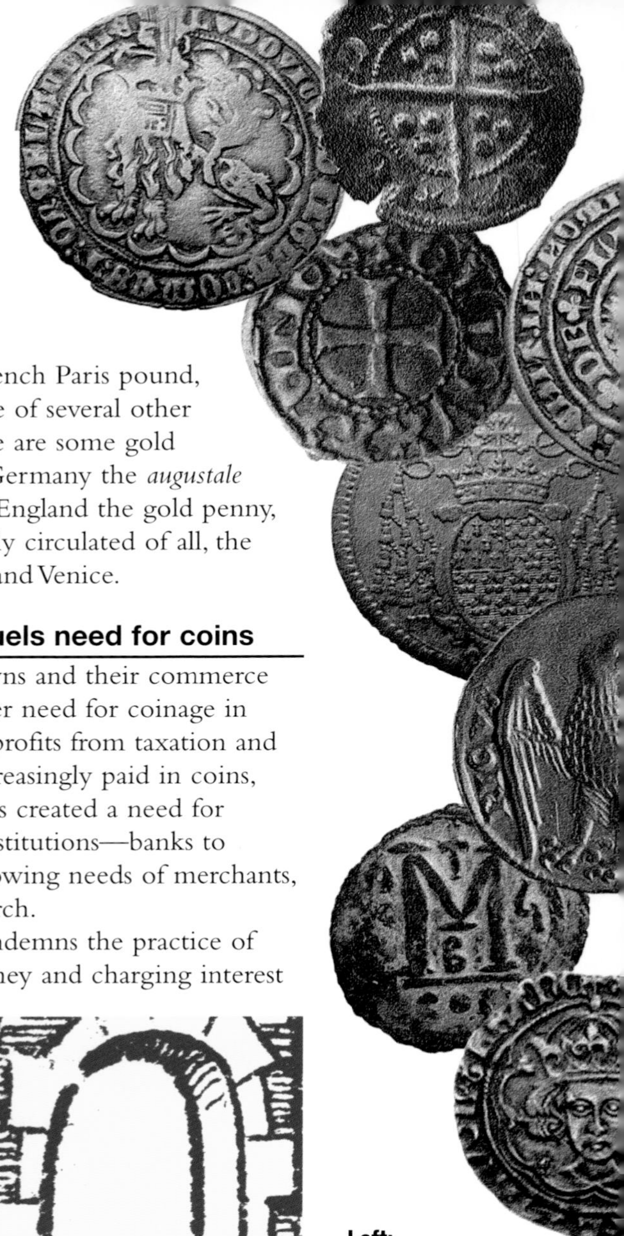

Many of the older European coins that were used by the nobility remain in circulation. These are made of gold or more commonly silver, and since they are worth their weight in the metal, it does not matter from which country they originate. Most of the silver for coinage comes from Saxony, where there are several rich mines.

The basic silver coin in circulation since Carolingian times is the *denarius* (originally the basic unit of the Roman monetary system). Twelve *denarii* make a *solidus*, or shilling; and 20 *soldii* make a *libra*, or pound. More recently, the *grossus denarius*, or "groat" has been introduced, worth several pennies. In Germany, a silver *mark* is worth 13 *soldii* and 4 *denarii*.

Regional and provincial currencies in circulation include the English pound sterling and the French Paris pound, together with those of several other French cities. There are some gold coins as well—in England the *augustale* (*see "Fact box"*), in England the gold penny, and the most widely circulated of all, the florin of Florence and Venice.

## Urban growth fuels need for coins

The growth of towns and their commerce has created a greater need for coinage in everyday use. The profits from taxation and feudal dues are increasingly paid in coins, and in turn, this has created a need for reliable financial institutions—banks to handle the ever growing needs of merchants, lords, and the Church.

The Church condemns the practice of usury (lending money and charging interest

**Left:**
A merchant uses a counting board to calculate how much he is worth at day's end.

**Fact box**

The gold German coin called the *augustale* remained in circulation for centuries. In the vernacular German language, its name became shortened into *thaler*, and from that the word "dollar" is derived.

**Above:** A French mint at work (left), while merchants of the town discuss business.

**Below:** The German banker Jakob Fugger.

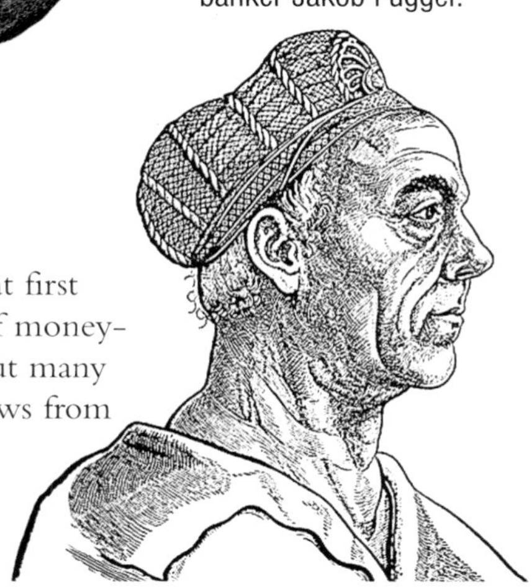

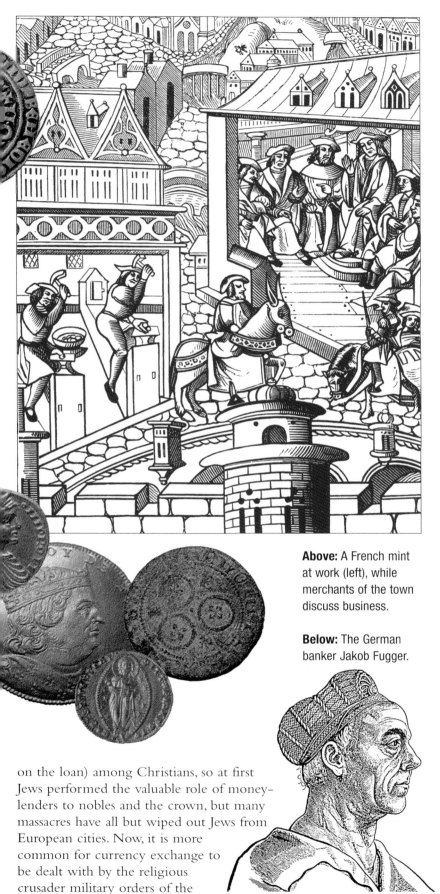

on the loan) among Christians, so at first Jews performed the valuable role of money-lenders to nobles and the crown, but many massacres have all but wiped out Jews from European cities. Now, it is more common for currency exchange to be dealt with by the religious crusader military orders of the Templars and the Hospitallers.

Given the military strength of these orders, their buildings are relatively safe from being robbed, and the piety of the orders' members mean that their honesty is supposed to be above reproach. Through their offices scattered across all of Europe, it is possible to pay large sums of money into one estate, and have an equal sum issued from a different estate in another kingdom. In this respect, they function as bankers, issuing letters of credit and supervising deposits, withdrawals, and cash transfers.

### The problem with usury

The Church prohibition of usury extends to payment of interest by a bank to clients who have deposited money. Medieval bankers get around this problem through an agreement known as a *commenda*. This involves one party providing capital for a venture, while the other guarantees a return on the investment. By paying interest on an investment rather than on a deposit (which the Church regards as a loan), no religious rules are broken.

Investment banking brings other benefits to the merchant through other services that the bank offers, such as temporary loans in the form of overdrafts and the ability to transfer funds from one place to another without the merchant needing to physically handle any money.

### Banks spring up

England, separated from the Continent, is not well placed to become a banking center. The biggest banks have developed in cities sited at the crossroads of Europe in northern Italy and Germany. A number of the larger Italian and Flemish banks maintain agreements with each other and with subsidiary financial houses in France, England, and Germany, principally those of the Fugger family.

Now, investors in one country can support ventures in another and kings can borrow money from banks in other countries. The growing complexity of international investment banking is making phenomenal wealth for banking families such as the Medicis of Florence and the German Fuggers of Augsburg.

# A Town's Trade and Commerce

In Europe, there is nothing approaching industry on a large scale except mining, and in most cases the typical artisan's workshop is a single small building.

As we have seen, craftsmen in towns employ one or more apprentices to help them, and many are members of guilds, protective institutions that ensure the quality of production within a town, regulate prices, and adjudicate in disputes between merchants or customers. Products often go through several workshops before completion, with each master working within his particular skill.

Merchants, bankers, or guilds act as agents, taking orders, allocating production quotas to the workshops, and then collecting the finished product and shipping it for a fee.

Towns and the immediate regions around them house a variety of craftsmen, apprentices, journeymen, and simple laborers.

## Old crafts

Leatherworking is one of the more important trades. Leather is used for a wide range of products from armor to door hinges, from buckets to fine bookbinding.

The processes of curing and tanning hides is the "dirty" end of the business, employing laborers for much of the stinky work, but once cured, hides are moved into the craftsmen's specialist workshops, where they are worked, fashioned, and decorated in many ways, depending on the finished product.

The best quality work may be found in horse saddles, fashionable belts, beautifully tooled book covers, sword scabbards, and all decorated with raised, stamped, or cut patterns, applied gold or silver filigree (fine wire) designs, and in many colors.

Metalworkers are always in demand, working in brass, bronze, iron, steel, and precious metals like silver and gold. There are specialists in armor and weaponry, horse brasses, pewterers who make drinking vessels and middle-class dining ware, silversmiths and goldsmiths who fashion fine jewelry, locksmiths, clock-makers for the churches (*see "Marking time"*), and bellfounders—church bells are in great demand.

Numerous smaller workshops make less glamorous metal items, such as nails, gate hinges and door handles, shoe studs, and farming implements.

Pottery workshops turn out vast quantities of domestic ware, from the cheapest to the most exquisite destined for the tables of the rich and noble. Glassware is making a comeback, especially in drinking vessels for wealthy merchants and for house windows, but the elite glassmakers are those who create the panels of stained glass for churches and cathedrals.

Other older crafts include hornworkers, plasterers, carpenters, sculptors in wood and stone, stonemasons, and textile spinners. However, in textiles cotton spinning has undergone a revolution as hand spinning with a "distaff spindle" is replaced by the spinning wheel. With the addition of a foot treadle for the spinner to power the wheel, cotton thread can be spun in a fraction of the time it used to take.

**Far left:** Detail of a saint sculpted in gold and silver.

**Left and above:** From the cover of a book of prayer, a silver brooch pin, and an earring with stones.

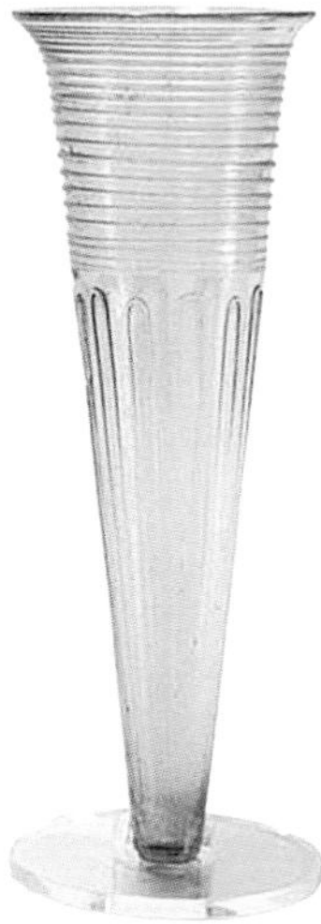

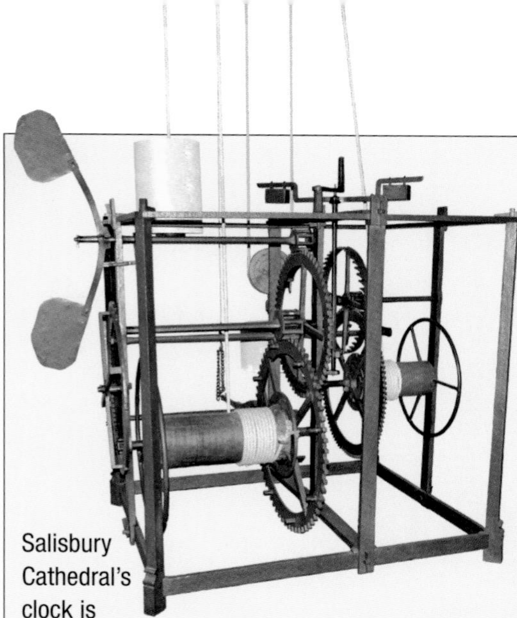

Salisbury Cathedral's clock is Europe's oldest (c.1386). Weights turn the cogs; with no face the time is told by ringing bells.

## Marking time

Once, only monks—with a day strictly divided between work and worship—needed to know the time. But a busy town finds commercial life hard to regulate properly if people turn up at different times through not knowing what hour of the day it is. Clocks, then, are no longer the preserve of monasteries. Many guildhalls and town halls, as well as parish churches, have installed the new mechanical clocks. With the clock, time becomes divided into regulated units, instead of remaining dependent on events or the day. While before the clock, people worked, ate, and slept according to the patterns of the sun and moon, now the day is presided over by a monitor from the time of rising to the hour of rest. Life has become a nine-to-five affair.

**Above:** Of all the different types of metal worker, the blacksmith is the most important tradesman, because of the number of items in daily use that need to be of forged metal.

**Right, top to bottom:** A medieval palm cup of colored glass; a clear glass cone beaker; a French pottery jug (smaller versions are used for drinking).

**Right and below:** A beautiful wood carving depicts the Twelve Apostles for a church altar; a French spinning wheel with a foot treadle.

**Above:** Mining deep requires the removal of water that can flood the tunnels.

## Mining—craft become industry

Mining, once a craft practiced by small family or cooperative units, is gradually becoming industrialized. In addition to the mining of iron ore, there has been an increase in the mining of other materials, including silver, lead, copper, gold, and anthracite coal.

Because of the demand for more ore, particularly precious metals for coins, a transition is taking place from a craft-based production to an expensive industry subject to central management. Instead of selling the ore to a forge, the miner is now typically an employee of the state or its agents.

As ore close to the ground is worked out, the mines are getting deeper and more difficult to work. The deepest mines tend to fill with water, which leads to the need for a pumping system. A variety of pumps, bucket chains, and treadmill devices are used, sometimes in combination with a waterwheel.

## A windmill

Like the traditional watermill, these more recently developed structures cleverly harness a force of nature—in this case wind—to make grinding corn an easier chore.

**1.** Sails turn the brake wheel (**2**). It turns the pinion (**3**), which turns the top millstone (**4**) to grind the corn.
**5.** Ground flour is collected in sacks.

## Lime burning

Lime is another mineral resource that—once dug in small amounts for use as a fertilizer—is now required in industrial quantities for the building trades and in fulling (*see page 88*). On the fields, lime improves soil structure and neutralizes excessive soil acidity, leading to increased crop yields.

With churches, cathedrals, schools, and guildhalls spring up everywhere, the demand for "quicklime," which is an essential ingredient in making mortar, has grown enormously. Quicklime is made by burning broken limestone in a lime-kiln.

Most lime-kilns are 10 or 12 feet in diameter, walled around to 3 or 4 feet high, with draft tunnels at the base. Inside the kiln a fire of brushwood is made and broken limestone added in alternate layers heaped to the top. The kiln is then covered with slabs of turf and left to burn for a week or two.

Inside, temperatures can reach as high as 1700°F. From time to time, the resulting lump lime is emptied from the bottom, which is a horrid job. The kilns radiate heat and fumes for yards around and lime burning is thirsty work. In addition, the dust is pungent to the nose and eyes, and injuries through asphyxiation are common. A quart of ale was often part of the payment for the lime-burner.

To make the powder form necessary for spreading on fields or making into mortar, the burnt lime is "slaked" by adding water to the still hot lumps. The reaction is extreme, and quicklime is a dangerous product. It can cause terrible burns on the skin and blindness if any fragment gets into the eyes.

**Below right:** A lime kiln.

**Right:** Alchemists—applying a mixture of mysticism, theology, and ancient Greek philosophy—seek perfection of form. Their weird apparatus frightens ordinary folk, who think they are magicians.

**Below:** An apothecary's shop is open for business, providing chemical and herbal medicines to doctors and the public.

## Alchemists

Alchemy is a relatively new "science" which was introduced into Europe at the time of the Crusades. The first alchemical texts were translated from Arabic into Latin. The alchemist's work is based on the four humors (*see pages 50–51*) derived from Aristotle's theory of earth, air, fire, and water. These elements are associated with phlegm, blood, yellow bile, and black bile. Unlike the apothecary, the alchemist practices his art with weirdly shaped instruments, magical incantations, codified symbols, and symbolic colors.

Alchemy is a mysterious and terrifying art to those unfamiliar with it—and that is almost everyone. The prime study of the alchemist is the search for moral perfection, which centers on discovering the legendary stone that can turn lead into pure gold.

In the eyes of the Church, this science is suspiciously heretical, since it appears to deny the power of God as the only being capable of creating moral perfection. Alchemists, therefore, are feared (even though people consult them when the need arises), and the writings of Aristotle have been banned by the pope.

## Apothecaries

Most towns have several apothecaries, who operate through a small retail shop at the front of their homes. As a skilled practitioner of pharmacy, the apothecary studies the properties of herbs and chemicals to make up curative ointments and potions, known as *materia medica*, which he dispenses to the public, doctors, and surgeons.

In addition to making medicines, the apothecary also offers general medical advice and a range of services, such as simple surgery and midwifery.

## A man of letters

In many respects, one of the more useful new trades of the Middle Ages is that of the professional letter writer. For some failed clerical students, setting out a stall in the market square and offering passersby their limited ability with words is the only hope of earning a living.

Letters might be required to act as a reference to a prospective employer, for an uneducated noble a romantic poem to his beloved, or for a dispossessed peasant a means of writing home (the letter to be deciphered by another letter writer at the destination).

There is no formal postal system, but many merchants or their junior staff are willing to carry dispatches from one town to another for a fee.

Illiterate folk rely on letter writers to pen any messages for them, and merchants to deliver their "post" abroad.

# The International Wool Trade

**Despite the finer and more exotic fabrics coming in larger quantities from the East via Italy, the largest single trade in the Middle Ages is the gathering and sale of wool.**

England's forests have been cleared to provide pasture land for sheep, whose wool is in high demand.

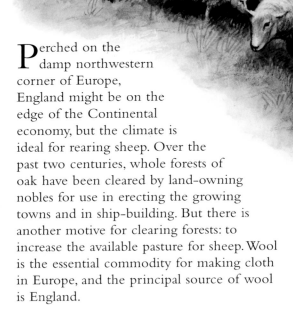

Perched on the damp northwestern corner of Europe, England might be on the edge of the Continental economy, but the climate is ideal for rearing sheep. Over the past two centuries, whole forests of oak have been cleared by land-owning nobles for use in erecting the growing towns and in ship-building. But there is another motive for clearing forests: to increase the available pasture for sheep. Wool is the essential commodity for making cloth in Europe, and the principal source of wool is England.

## Clearing the forests

The heavy rainfall produces luxurious pastures ideal for grazing sheep and so England is able to produce fine quality wool in great quantity. However, the skilled craftsmen to make high-quality cloth are few and far between in England. These are found in Flanders where, in the lower, water-sodden ground, sheep do not flourish.

As a result, the majority of English wool is exported to Flanders, and the finished cloth imported as ready-made garments or blankets, or natural cloth ready for dyeing and making up. However, several merchants resent paying Flemish weavers for their work and in England there is a growing number of factories handling all the stages of wool production.

This is one of the main reasons why so many peasants are moving into the new towns springing up on wool-trade wealth, where they become a source of cheap labor for burghers. Some peasants even find work in the wool trade, although in one of the least pleasant jobs.

## The fuller

Cloth made from recently sheared sheep is not fit to sell because of the grease and impurities in it—first it must be fulled. This is done by placing the "tardage" of cloth into large vats filled with a noxious mixture of stale urine, slaked lime, and "fullers' earth" (aluminum oxide).

The fuller then follows the woolen bales into the vat and stomps on them for hours. The stench is almost unbearable and the job is mind-numbingly tedious. Even so, the fuller must not fail in concentration because the process also tightens the weave and thickens the cloth. If it is not treated evenly for exactly the right amount of time, the whole bale might be ruined.

Once the cloth is ready, it is rinsed in clean water and stretched out to dry on a "tenterframe." Some merchants are erecting fulling mills on riverbanks, benefiting both from the plentiful supply of clean water, and also using its power to drive engines that do the stomping instead of peasant fullers.

**Below:** The fuller's dirty, tiring work transforms woven raw wool into valuable cloth that will eventually be sold all over Europe.

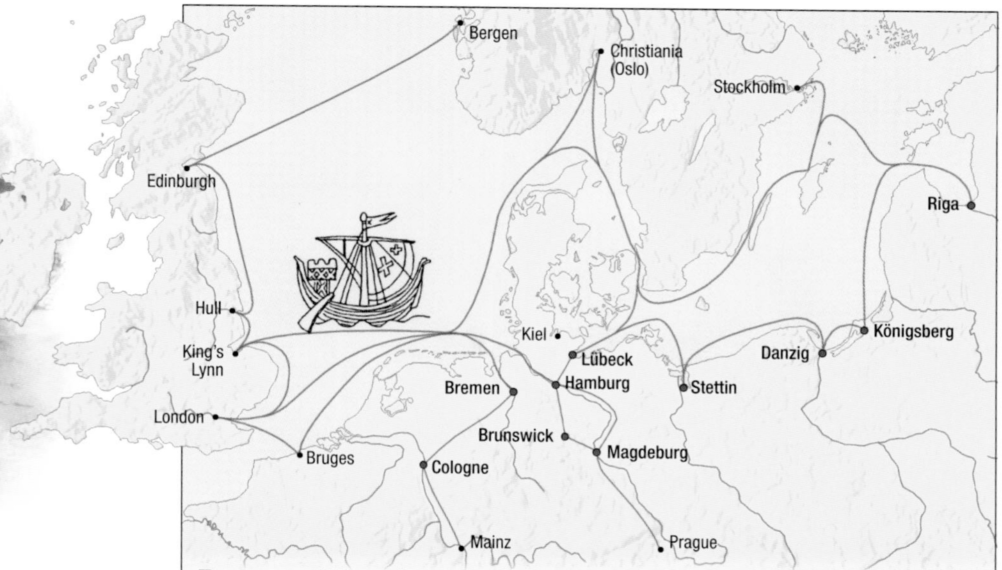


## Everyone gets a cut

The state also demands its share of the wool trade by imposing the "Staple," a tax on all woolen transactions. In order to ensure that the tax is collected, the king restricts wool exporting to a few Staple ports. The most important on the English coast is Sandwich, and on the French coast Calais, which—because it is in English hands—means the king receives an export and an import tax on each wool bale.

All across the south and center of England, towns are expanding on the wealth of the wool trade. The churches grow even richer on their increased tithes, and many small-town churches have been enlarged to sometimes cathedral-like proportions.

## Power of the Hanseatic League.

Although by no means heavily involved in the wool trade, the Hanseatic League is one of the major players in the import and export of European cloth. The Hanseatic League was originally formed by the northern towns of Hamburg and Lübeck in the 12th century.

The major source of Hansa income is derived from the vast demand for fish, with is a large part of the Christian diet. As fish does not keep well, it needs to be salted. Lübeck has access to Baltic fish, but no salt, whereas Hamburg has no fish (the North Sea being too difficult for industrial fishing), but plenty of salt from the massive salt mines at nearby Kiel.

From these beginnings, the Hanseatic League has spread to include most cities of northern Germany and the Baltic. It is not so much a league of cities as it is an international guild of merchant associations within the cities. As a consequence, the league's fleet of mercantile ships has expanded to be the largest in Europe.

The crowns of most northern European countries have granted the Hansa the right to send an agent to operate in their major cities and ports. The agents' power is considerable because the Hansa have a virtual monopoly on the transport and sale of salt, herring, grain, timber, honey, amber, ships' stores, and other bulk commodities. Those operating in England, France, and Flanders also play a large part in the lucrative wool trade, benefiting from the numerical superiority of Hansa ships and the superior quality of the innovative ship, the Baltic cog (*see page 93*).

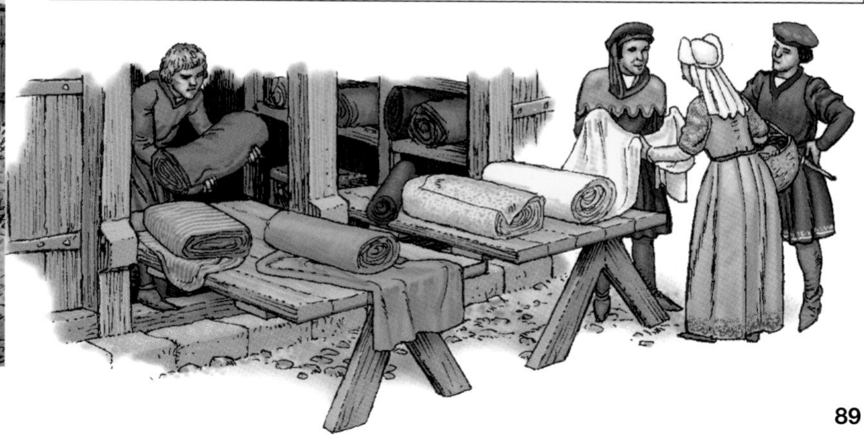

## The Rigors of the Journey

**As villages grow into towns and towns into cities, trade—the lifeblood of the merchant burghers—needs good communications, but roads of the Middle Ages are poor.**

Travel in the Middle Ages is slow, uncomfortable, and usually dangerous. Not many paved Roman roads remain in even poor condition, and most ways are mere dirt tracks that turn into a river of mud when it rains. Potholes, mud, and subsidence restricts travel to walking, horses, and light two-wheeled carts, pulled by ox, horse, donkey, or most likely by hand.

When a journey has to be made, most people walk. Horses are very expensive and only the rich can afford them. Even on horseback, a rider can only expect to travel about 20 miles in a long day, if the weather is fine and dry.

### Stand and deliver!

The open country between small villages and towns may be infested by outlaws, escaped convicted criminals operating alone or in small bands, who pounce on the unwary traveler, robbing and killing indiscriminately. Therefore, it is hardly a surprise that commoners rarely move around, sometimes never traveling more than a few miles from the place where they were born.

The most traffic on the dirt tracks consists of the more mobile nobility with their armed retinues, groups of pilgrims in bands large enough to deter robbers, and merchants, usually in a mutually defensive caravan. Even so, substantial journeys are usually made by river and sea to avoid long and dangerous overland routes.

## The cost of travel

The worsened condition of the roads and the great danger of meeting robbers in the half-light discourages travel in the dark and rainy winter months. Similarly, only the most desperate or confidently well-armed will take to the high roads at night.

Given the poor quality and endurance of wheeled vehicles on the rutted roads, the transportation of choice is the packhorse, or mule. Since a single animal can only carry a relatively low weight of goods, it is usual to see several, tied together in a line, wending their slow way along the roads.

Merchants try to avoid the better main roads for the simple reason that every time they encounter a bridge or a crossroads, there is sure to be a local lord's toll to pay, adding to the cost of the goods. On the other hand, lesser tracks may be overrun by bandits.

## Separate tracks for the livestock

Along the ridges of the countryside there exists an alternative road system, one that is not much used for ordinary traveling from one place to another. These are the "drove roads," tracks made by tradition for driving livestock to market.

Travelers follow the course of what was once a Roman road, of which only scraps of paving are now visible (*front left*). They are headed for the town in the distance (*right*), beyond which the sea can be glimpsed. In the valley below, river craft carry goods toward a port for shipping abroad. On the crest of the hills (*back left*), cattle are driven to the town's market along a "drove road."

**Far left:** An unlucky, lone traveler "chooses" to surrender his money rather than his life to the highwaymen who have pounced on him.

The routes generally keep to the crest of hills, which gives the drovers a good clear view of where they are headed and also keeps the flocks and herds out of the more crowded valleys. Drove roads have wide grass banks, bordered by hedges, where the cattle or sheep can graze when they spend the night on route.

## Taking to the rivers

The growth in international trade has led to the building of new ports and enlargement of older ones. In most cases, these are sited at the mouths of rivers, which give access to the hinterland by barges. River transportation is more efficient than by road. Few men are needed to man a barge capable of carrying 20–30 times as much as a wagon or a pack train. And the journey down to the sea is usually fast, aided by the current.

On arrival at the river's estuary, it is a simple matter to maneuver the barge alongside an ocean-going ship ready to load the goods. No wonder the ports of Europe are becoming the powerhouses of trade, and shipping company owners, once mere salty sailors of a single vessel, are fast turning into a new seafaring middle class of their own.

# The Medieval Port

The principal business of a port is given by its name, which derives from the Old French-Latin word, meaning doorway, or gateway. Through these portals flows the wealth of kings in taxes and merchants in profits.

**Right:** A mariner's astrolabe is used to figure out the latitude of a ship at sea.

Ports are important centers for trade, commerce, the creation of money, and a country's military security. As a result, few remain outside of royal control.

Granted a king's charter, a port can expect to expand greatly, even influencing the region immediately behind it, including other towns and villages. In return, the port's burghers must bear a large financial burden in making sure its defenses are adequate in scale and properly manned.

The best harbors are those with a natural basin, with headlands protecting against bad weather, or those sited within a river estuary, such as London, Bristol, Rouen, Le Havre, and Hamburg. Whatever the site, the wooden jetties standing on their massive timber piles are a constant hive of daily activity as ships' masters wait to catch the next tide to sail.

## Finding the way

Few sea journeys are extended because the world is flat and any sailor venturing too far out from land might sail straight over the edge into the endless void.

**Above:** Cogs being unloaded in a busy northern European port. Simple manpower is backed by a treadwheel crane, just one sign of the technological advances being made in the shipping trade.

Navigation in the Middle Ages is not very advanced and aside from a crude compass and perhaps an astrolabe, there are no navigation aids. Consequently most sailing is done in view of the coastline following the guide in the Book of the Sea, which gives directions based on the silhouette of headlands and "soundings," measurements of the depth at those points.

This means that northern European ports generally communicate with one another, as do those of the Mediterranean, but there is little sea trade between the two regions. Goods from Italy tend to be taken overland, where the roads are in a better state.

Nevertheless, merchants bring back many luxuries from far off places. From Africa, slaves, sugar, gold, ivory, and precious stones; from Asia, silk, furs, carpets, and valuable spices such as pepper, cinnamon, and nutmeg. These exotics have traveled from the other end of the world along the fabled Silk Road and the Spice Route to reach the ports of the eastern Mediterranean.

Dominating eastern Mediterranean mercantile trade, the Venetians and their rivals the Genoese transport rice, cotton, perfume, mirrors, lemon, and melons. On the North Sea and Baltic fringes, the Hanseatic League dominates with a large fleet of innovative cargo ships called cogs.

## A bulk carrier

The Baltic cog is a highly specialized cargo carrier. Its predecessor, the Viking *knorr*, while highly seaworthy, could only carry a limited amount of cargo. A cog can carry up to 20 times as much cargo. It is "clinker built"—from a series of overlapping planks fastened to a series of cross-frames—with a flat bottom and a centrally mounted stern rudder. This gives far more steering control than the traditional sweep oars of the *knorr*.

A cog can be fitted with a removable keel and hold one mast with a square rigged sail. With its flat bottom, the cog is well suited to sailing in shallow waters and can reach most riverine ports with ease.

## A great risk of loss

Merchants and the seamen that sail their ships take great risks. Storms at sea are a constant terror and the danger of piracy is very real. Should sailors become shipwrecked on a coast, they have little hope of rescue. Most countries' nautical laws state that all loot recovered from a shipwrecked vessel is the property of the finders, unless there are survivors—so it is in the interests of the finders to make sure there are none.

Because of the dangers involved with shipping cargoes, it is a common practice for merchants to form partnerships and have each partner buy a share of a cargo or a ship. By spreading their investment over several cargoes and shipping them on several ships, the risk of a catastrophic loss is reduced. Meeting places for these partnerships can be found at all the ports.

## Toward a new horizon, new worlds

Despite the dangers and expense of sea travel, some merchants, especially those of Spain and Portugal, are eager for their ships' masters to take greater risks and sail further than ever before. Those beginning to probe southward along the West African coast are discovering new markets, and discovering many extraordinary things.

They are opening the way for sailors of the future to venture beyond the edges of the world, to the Americas, and even as far as legendary China and Japan.

# Glossary

**Angevin** Dynasty from Anjou, southwestern France, also known as the Plantagenets, whose Geoffrey IV conquered *Normandy* in 1144.

**astrolabe** A disc-shaped navigational device, possibly invented in 2nd century BCE Greece. Its pointer is used to measure the angles of stars from a ship's current position. The vessel's latitude and longitude can then be calculated if the date and time of day are known.

**bailey** A courtyard or enclosed area surrounding a castle, defined by a ditch and *palisade*.

**ballista** A large crossbow used to attack a castle.

**Barbarian Codes** Methods that settle feuds, which involve the defendant convincing others to take up his oath of innocence (compurgation), surviving a physical ordeal, or fighting his enemy.

**boss** The round- or cone-shaped metal lump riveted to the center of a shield, sometimes with decoration.

**burgher** A middle-class inhabitant of a town, who works as a merchant or businessman.

**canonization** The process where (usually) the pope makes someone a saint for their good work and holiness while they were alive.

**chapter house** The meeting room of a monastery, church, or cathedral, sometimes a separate building.

**chivalry** Derived from "cheval," the French word for "horse," it is the code of conduct the medieval knight is supposed to follow.

**cog** A style of ship with superior maneuverability and cargo capacity, compared to the knorr type of vessel it replaced.

**croft** A small piece of land farmed by a *villein*, who rents it by working for his lord for part of the week.

**Crusades** From the French "croisade," to mark with the Cross—a series of eight wars beginning in 1096 where Christians of western Europeans went to reclaim Jerusalem and the Holy Land from Muslims, but also fought to gain territory in the region. They deteriorated with the Fourth Crusade, when Venice directed the assault toward the Byzantine capital of Constantinople in 1204, and ended in 1291 with failed attempts to regain Syria.

**curtain walls** Tall stone walls that form the outer defense of a castle, with a number of taller, projecting mural towers from where they can be defended.

**destrier** The warhorse of a knight, derived from the Latin "dexter," or the right, since the knight's *squire* led the horse with his right hand.

**diocese** An administrative territory of the Roman Catholic Church, also called a bishopric or *see*.

**donjon** A defensive tower or keep at the center of a castle, from which "dungeon" is derived.

**doublet** A closely-fitted tunic with a skirt-like bottom, sometimes without sleeves and often in combination with hose (tights or stockings).

**excommunication** Exclusion from Christian society, although it is possible for the offender to repent and be allowed back into the community.

**feudal system** A system where *fealty*—an oath of loyalty—is given to someone in return for property, such as a minor lord and his peasants being given land to work on and paying for the privilege by fighting on behalf of their superior lord when the need arises.

**fief** An estate or piece of land held by someone in return for their support of a superior person.

**flax** A type of herb. Its fibers are used to make cloth.

**Franks** The people of Germany who spread through western Europe from the 3rd century AD, leading to the formation of the *Holy Roman Empire*. The country of France and Franconia region of Germany take their names from the Franks who once dominated them.

**fuller** Someone who cleans and prepares wool or cloth before it is made into a garment.

**harrow** A type of rake used to cover seeds with soil after land has been plowed and planted.

**hennin** A tall, conical or heart-shaped hat worn by women, also called a steeple headdress.

**Holy Roman Empire** The empire of the *Franks*, which began CE 800 when the pope made Charlemagne, head of the Carolingian dynasty, a "Roman emperor." Under the Habsburg dynasty of Austria, the Holy Roman Empire dominated central Europe and Spain in the 15th–18th centuries. Emperor Francis II gave up the title in 1806 under pressure from the conquering Napoleon of France.

**hundreds** Groups of ten *tithings*—a total of a hundred families—and the land they occupy.

**indulgences** People who make these payments to the Church are deemed free of sin, thus avoiding years in *purgatory* when they die.

**journeyman** A qualified member of a trade. The more skilled become masters, who can teach apprentices and employ journeymen of their own.

**landsknecht** A mercenary foot soldier from Germany, armed with a pike or halberd (a pole with a metal blade/spike on the end).

**Lombards** Germanic people who invaded Italy in CE 568 and settled in a region that became the kingdom of **Lombardy**. When the Lombards threatened Rome in the 8th century, the pope summoned the *Franks* and Charlemagne (r.768–814) conquered Lombardy in 774.

**machicolation** A projecting gallery that juts out at the top of a castle wall on supports called corbels. Holes allow objects to be dropped onto enemies scaling the wall.

**medieval** Something from the Middle Ages period, generally CE 800–1450.

**Moors** North African muslims who spread west and north to Spain and southern France. They clashed with native Christians and were finally defeated by Spain in 1492.

**motte** The raised mound on which a keep or castle stands, surrounded by at least one *bailey*.

**Normans** "Northmen" or "Norsemen," Vikings who raided the coast of Europe in the 9th–10th centuries CE and established the Duchy of **Normandy**, from where they settled in southern Italy and Sicily and conquered England in 1066.

**ordination** The ceremony where a man is made a priest.

**palisade** A wooden fence surrounding a castle, usually on the embankment of earth made when a defensive ditch is dug around a *bailey*. Later castles had *curtain walls*.

**purgatory** The place where a deceased person is believed to suffer to pay for the sins they committed while alive. When purged of sin they are allowed into Heaven.

**reeve** The guardian or manager of a lord's manor or *fief*.

**Renaissance** "Rebirth," the 15–16th century period of European history when art, culture, science, and banking developed, beginning in Italy and spreading across Europe.

**Saxons** Germans from Jutland who raided the North Sea in the 3rd–4th centuries CE. They settled in Gaul (France) but *Franks* drove them out in the 5th century. Some went to England and became the dominant race, while others formed the Duchy of Saxony near their homeland and continued to fight the Franks.

**scutage** If a knight can afford to pay scutage tax to his lord, he does not have to serve in his lord's battles.

**see** Or episcopal see, it is a *diocese* but can also refer to the office or position held by a bishop.

**serf** A peasant of the *feudal system*, who must work on a particular *fief* to earn shelter or to earn a knight's protection in times of war. Serfs are considered the property of the person who owns the land.

**shire** A group of *hundreds*. The land they occupy is equivalent to a *fief*. The person who looks after it is a *shire reeve,* or sheriff.

**solar** The room in a castle used as a bedroom by the lord and lady.

**squire** A young noble who has served as a page to a lord and from the age of 14 assists a knight, in the hope of becoming one himself when he is 21.

**sumptuary laws** Restrictions on the style of clothing a person may wear.

**tithe** A tax of about one tenth (tithe) of a peasant's earnings to their local church, in the form of grain, livestock, or farm produce.

**tithing** A group of ten local families.

**trebuchet** A type of giant catapult, which uses a counterweight to power a slingshot arm.

**vassal** In the *feudal system*, someone who has been granted a *fief* in return for loyalty to their overlord.

**vernacular** The native language of a country or region.

**villein** From the French for "village dweller," a different word for *serf*.

**wattle and daub** A type of construction where mud (daub) is plastered over a frame of sticks (wattle) to form a wall.

**wimple** A cloth or scarf that covers a woman's head, its end gathered around her chin.

**winnowing** A harvest process where the light chaff or husks are allowed to blow away to separate it from the grain.

**yeoman** Someone who owns a small farm, between a *villein* and a knight/noble in the class system. In war, yeomen fought as foot soldiers.

# Index